THE IMPATIENT LIBERTARIAN
WHICH ROAD AHEAD?

Ron Manners AO

Published by Wilkinson Publishing Pty Ltd
ACN 006 042 173
PO Box 24135, Melbourne, VIC 3001, Australia
Ph: +61 3 9654 5446
enquiries@wilkinsonpublishing.com.au
www.wilkinsonpublishing.com.au

WilkinsonPublishing

wilkinsonpublishinghouse

WPBooks

Mannwest Group Pty Ltd
Hayek on Hood
3/31 Hood Street
Subiaco (Perth)
Western Australia 6008
Tel: +61 8 9382 1288
Email: mannwest@mannkal.org
Web: www.mannwest.com

© Copyright Ron Manners 2024

All rights reserved. No part of this publication may be reproduced, stored in a retrieval system or transmitted in any form by any means without the prior permission of the copyright owner. Enquiries should be made to the publisher.

Every effort has been made to ensure that this book is free from error or omissions. However, the Publisher, the Authors, the Editor or their respective employees or agents, shall not accept responsibility for injury, loss or damage occasioned to any person acting or refraining from action as a result of material in this book whether or not such injury, loss or damage is in any way due to any negligent act or omission, breach of duty or default on the part of the Publisher, the Authors, the Editor, or their respective employees or agents.

Title: The Impatient Libertarian (Which Road Ahead?)
ISBN: 9781922810281 – Softcover
       9781922810298 – Hardcover

1.Economics 2. Australian History 3. Gold mines, nickel mines & mining – Western Australia: Kalgoorlie region – history 4. Personal narratives – Australian. 5. Kalgoorlie – history. Manners, Ron (Ronald B). 6. Banking investment, economic aspects – Australia. 7. Politics.

Design by Michael Bannenberg.
Cover Photo Provided by: Atlas Network Liberty Forum.
New York City, 16 Nov 2023.

Printed and bound in Australia by Ligare Pty Ltd.

CONTENTS

Preface	v
Introduction by Laurie P. Morrow, Ph.D.	ix

PART 1

Hope for the Future	1
Packing Paper Revelations – Leonard E. Read	7
The Unspeakable 'Evil' Textbook – Prof. John Hospers	15
No Philosopher Prince – HRH Prince Philip, The Duke of Edinburgh	25
Knowledge? Not A Problem – Prof. F.A. Hayek	33
The Triumph of the Egg Smuggler – Sir Antony Fisher AFC	43
All Five – All Different, Any Consistent Characteristics?	45

PART 2

Life: One Accident After Another! – Developing an Art Form?	49
Pom Pom's Clarinet	53
Why were Ukraine's President Zelensky's Senior Politicians and Economic Advisers Zooming into our Office in Perth, on 28 June, 2022?	63

PART 3

The Free Market Road Show (Europe's Eighth Wonder of the World)	87
A Three City Sampler:	
• Tallinn – Estonia – The Home of Entrepreneurship	89
• Bratislava – Talking of Energy	99
• Warsaw – Kyiv – Economic Reforms (Rebuilding an Economy)	109

PART 4

Australia at the Crossroads in 2024	119
BE AN ACTIVIST! Much more fun than being a spectator	129
Conclusion	138

Afterword	139
Acknowledgements	141
Index	143

PREFACE

Having prospered and enjoyed the benefits of life as an Australian citizen, I am mindful of my good fortune, and I want all future Australians to enjoy as much of all that the best law and culture can offer. I want others to have the same life-changing benefits that I have had from exposure to the libertarian philosophy of self-responsibility and a reluctance to become a burden on others, including taxpayers, many of whom are already struggling to pay their way.

However, there appears to be little appreciation of why Australia offers so much, or of the pitfalls that occur when Australians depart from the practices that have created our opportunities. I endowed *Mannkal Economic Education Foundation* in the belief and hope that it will contribute an understanding, of these benefits, to young and yet unborn Australians.

The best years for Australia are ahead of us but only if we continue to invest in the brightest minds of the next generation. Circumstances may change, over time, but my objectives are quite specific both concerning the kind of society that will best serve our future and how Mannkal should contribute. I expect all those who share responsibility for Mannkal to be guided by these aims.

Australia has, until recently, been a relatively free society allowing individuals more room to manage their own affairs within stable and common law that avoids favouritism and protects life, liberty and property. As anyone may observe, these virtues are practiced most in countries to which refugees flee and least in countries from which they escape.

The relative success of governments that trespass only lightly on their citizens' liberty is evident and supported by theory. Austrian economists, especially F.A. Hayek, have demonstrated, to my satisfaction, that even the most benign governments could never assemble the information or command the administrative machinery to serve the diverse and ever-changing interests and aptitudes of the millions of their people. Governments too often exceed their legitimate roles, preventing people from planning and managing their own lives. As Hayek himself said in *The Counter-Revolution of Science (p 162)*:

His [a merchant's] special knowledge is almost entirely knowledge of particular circumstances of time or place, or, perhaps, a technique of ascertaining those circumstances in a given field. But though this knowledge is not of a kind which can be formulated in generic propositions or acquired once and for all. Though in an age of Science it is for that reason regarded as knowledge of an inferior kind, it is for all practical purposes no less important than scientific knowledge. And while it is perhaps conceivable that all theoretical knowledge might be combined in the heads of a few experts and thus made available to a single central authority, it is this knowledge of the particular, of the fleeting circumstances of the moment and of local conditions, which will never exist otherwise than dispersed among many people.

Further, experience tells us that few governments remain consistently benign. Lord Acton once observed that power tends to corrupt and the Public Choice theorists have explained how concentrated vested interests divert democratic governments' policies from the general interest to those focused special interests, at the expense of people with less ability to organise. Nevertheless, people respond to the good or bad arguments of good or bad opinion leaders, and it is of the nature of democracy that their governments follow. Good or at least better government is not a utopian dream but will be achieved only by constant questioning from alert and vigilant citizens. Without constant pruning, governments will continue to grow. We have allowed governments to grow to such an extent that an appropriate form of pruning may be to start hacking at the roots.

The idea for this book first came from my good friend Laurie Morrow who after reading one of my recent speeches sent me a short note recommending that I expand my thoughts into a short book. She said,

What would make this book especially valuable is that

there seems to be an unspoken assumption that a model like Leonard Read's is the "One True Model" to which all who would inspire must conform. It's a brilliant model – but it's not suited to all temperaments or circumstances. The temptation, especially for younger readers, is to try to force themselves into a clearly successful mould that's ill-suited to their personality or situation. How liberating – how inspiring – to be presented with at least four other, proven approaches to successful economic leadership – to know one can be a Prince Philip in thorny circumstances and still "get the job done" – and done brilliantly! Or that the more retiring role of the philosopher-teacher can be at least as effective as being an activist mounting the bulwarks in the public eye.

All five types are effective – done right. And all five are needed. Dr. Johnson said, of Paradise Lost, "None ever wished it longer." Well, had Dr. Johnson read Ron's essay, he'd have wanted it longer, indeed!

So, armed with such encouragement, I set to work to bring you this, my eighth book. You may note that the leaders I describe in the following pages as influential to me are all men. I am finding however, as I proceed through life, that these days I am far more influenced by women, such that a complimentary book to this one, may one day be written.

Ron Manners AO, 10 Feb 2024

INTRODUCTION

By Laurie P. Morrow, Ph.D., CAP®

Recently, I read an essay of Ron's reflecting on the leadership styles of five leaders, men whose work, in recent years, helped advance free society and encourage governments to be responsive rather than intrusive. It was their work that inspired Ron to create the Mannkal Economic Education Foundation.

This essay was one of Ron's finest, and it also seemed a discussion in embryo of some larger work. It was thus with delight that I opened an email from Ron to find a draft of *The Impatient Libertarian* – the book that brief essay promised. In this book, Ron presents compelling accounts of how men with vastly different personalities, circumstances, and strategies successfully addressed threats to liberty. One would have to work hard, indeed, to find sources of inspiration who, though committed to the common goal of advancing liberty, differed so much from each other.

There's Leonard Read, whose essay about a pencil – *https://fee.org/resources/i-pencil/* rewrote economics for millions of people of all ages around the world, and, of course, F.A. Hayek, who taught the world to read the language and 'signals' of 'price fluctuation'.

Then, there's John Hospers, the philosopher who sat upon a hill and dreamed not of the death of kings, but of the death of communism – and who inspired others to strive for that same goal.

Among my favorite chapters is "The Triumph of the Egg Smuggler," on Sir Antony Fisher, the fighter pilot turned entrepreneur turned economic revolutionary (why, one wonders, has no one yet made a movie based on this remarkable life?).

Another major influence in Ron's life, was Austrian Economist F.A. Hayek. As was customary for Hayek, he left a little piece of himself with everyone with whom he engaged. In this way the free-market movement is not a fan club for dead economists, but a thriving community of younger people carrying with them the fertile intellectual underpinnings left by their exposure to Hayek.

Hayek's understanding of the human condition, his discussions on humility and hubris (the fatal conceit, as he called it) highlighted the challenges of responsibility. He expanded on these themes in his book *The Constitution of Liberty* where, on page 72 he says: –

"This denial of responsibility is, however, commonly due to a fear of responsibility, a fear that necessarily also becomes a fear of freedom. It is doubtless because the opportunity to build one's own life also means an unceasing task, a discipline that man must impose upon himself if he is to achieve his aims, that many people are afraid of liberty."

And last, but certainly not least, is "No Philosopher Prince," on His Royal Highness, the late Prince Philip. A man of action, not words, of passionate commitment rather than nuanced debate, having endured a childhood riddled by want and danger, he understood in his bones the importance of freedom and the destructive potential of unchecked government and proved himself, time and again, an unexpected champion of economic freedom.

All these men advanced the cause of liberty while remaining true to themselves, drawing upon their individual strengths and weaknesses and frustrations and victories to make the world freer. May their stories inspire us to forge in our own souls such a legacy of freedom.

Laurie P. Morrow, Ph.D., CAP®
Vermont, USA 31 July 2023

PART 1

HOPE FOR THE FUTURE

After my return from the 2021 Mont Pelerin Society events in Guatemala, some thoughts were rattling around in my mind. Let me share some of those thoughts with you.

For the first week in Guatemala, I was engaged in board training. I must say the Mont Pelerin Society board is the most interesting board that has been my pleasure on which to serve. I have been confronted with a real-life board as was described by one of the greatest management gurus, Tom Peters, in his book *Liberation Management*. Tom Peters was greatly influenced by Hayekian structures, and his views on management could be described as "achieving much more by doing less".

Tom Peters acknowledged Hayek's influence, by dedicating the book to F.A. Hayek.

The second week I participated in the Mont Pelerin Society General Meeting, where we were hosted by the University Francisco Marroquin (UFM), one of the most outstanding universities in the world. One of their secrets 'for success' at UFM is to accept absolutely no government funding whatsoever. This formula, based purely on high academic standards and merit, works.

During that conference week I was continually reminded of the number of successful Mannkal Scholars who have become permanent team members at the many host think tanks around the world. At one evening event, I was asked to expand on the five main influences behind the creation of our Mannkal Foundation and will share those thoughts with you here.

You may already know the five individuals who have affected me the most, their influence deeply embedded into Mannkal. They are Leonard Read, the Founder of the Foundation for Economic Education and one of the founders of the Mont Pelerin Society; Professor John Hospers, philosopher, teacher, and author of many books; Prince Philip, Duke of Edinburgh, and instigator of the Commonwealth Study Conferences; Nobel Prize winning Austrian economist and philosopher Professor F.A. Hayek; and Sir Antony Fisher, businessman and founder of the Institute of Economic Affairs and the Atlas Network.

Now, so many years later as I reflect upon the influence each of these individuals wielded, I have come to the realisation that the five were totally different in their style and execution. Hence, the inspiration for this book. Each of the five main influencers can be categorised according to the degree that they focussed on philosophy (ideas) versus strategy. I have ranked them according to my own perceptions of how their individual styles meet this criterion by allocating percentages of philosophy and economics on the one hand versus strategy on the other.

With my engineering background I am always seeking to measure our progress here at Mannkal, on a regular basis. So, how are we doing right now and into the future? In the river of life, you will be challenged with tributaries from time to time, but the longer-term rewards go to those who stay connected to the program on a long-term basis.

Now, as a concrete example of that, I would like to share with you an email I just received from one of our former Mannkal Scholars, from 2017, T.P., who interned with the Foundation for Economic Education (FEE) in Atlanta - December of 2017 through to February 2018 after attending the Mont Pelerin Society (MPS) meeting in South Korea in May 2017.

T.P. emailed me, as follows and, I share it, with his permission:

Ron, I am reaching out to let you know the influence Mannkal has had on my life views and career. I have, since moved out of Perth, and into the heart of government in Canberra working as a consultant on infrastructure projects. I have since been able to see how inefficient government is at allocating capital and hope to make a continuous difference.

I always remember the ideas learnt and free market views through my time at MPS South Korea and Foundation for Economic Education in Atlanta.

I am reaching out to continue learning about free market ideals and would like to become a member of the Mont Pelerin Society having attended the one in Seoul, South Korea. Would you kindly be able to nominate me for the membership?

Also, I would like to continue to be a Mannkal Ambassador and if there's anyone I can meet in Canberra happy to touch base."

To our Mannkal Scholars I would say that there will be times in your own careers, perhaps several years hence, when a thought that may have been rattling around in your mind during your Mannkal experience, suddenly clicks and you realise that it has a very clear relevance to your present situation. When this happens, I invite you to get back in contact with us at any time. Mannkal is a long- term project.

So why am I "impatient" you may ask? Despite the impeccable work of the five influencers, I mentioned above, we see all around us governments growing in scope, national debt soaring and entitlement and authoritarianism on the rise, both here in the West and elsewhere. We know that individual liberty and economic freedom is the basis of prosperity and well-being, and yet we see these principles denigrated as "selfish" or "right-wing". We see certain people – politicians in particular – stuck "on the wrong tram" unable to hold back from advocating for spending vast quantities of our future generation's earnings to repay the crippling debt they have accumulated whilst buying votes to remain 'in power'.

In the following pages, I go deeper into the leadership styles of my main five influencers. By examining the leadership styles of those that have gone before us, we can renew our efforts in more productive ways and remain inspired and "impatient" for a better future.

ANOTHER EXAMPLE OF MANNKAL SCHOLAR COMMUNICATIONS

"I recently came across a British writer whose quote resounded with the book you wrote, *The Lonely Libertarian*. "Loneliness truly is the tax we have to pay to atone for a certain complexity of mind." — *Alan De Botton*

I thought I'd email this to you as it involves philosophy in its first instance, but also economics to some extent when you start to dissect the meaning of 'tax' with 'complexity'. I personally, believe that reaching such a complexity of mind in life does not necessarily lead to loneliness but understand in some cases it might." H.K. - 2023

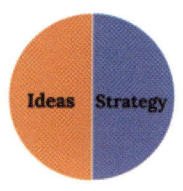

PACKING PAPER REVELATIONS

**Leonard E. Read –
Founder of the Foundation for
Economic Education (FEE) in 1946.**

I always talk about Leonard E. Read's influence on me before anyone else's, simply because, other than my parents', Leonard had the earliest impact on the development of my philosophical thinking that really got started when I was sixteen years old. This influence began unexpectedly when I stumbled upon Leonard's writing by pure chance.

At the age of sixteen I was still living with my parents in Kalgoorlie, and after school, I would help out at my father's mining engineering business, unpacking big machinery crates of Timken roller bearings from Ohio, USA. One time, as I was clearing away the packing materials, I noticed that it was crumpled pages from a magazine. This sparked my curiosity.

I took the crumpled pages home, and later that night smoothed them out to find that they were pages of *The Freeman magazine* published by the Foundation for Economic Education (FEE). The owner of Timken must have been an avid FEE supporter, as I saw that he had attached a circulation list to the front page of one of the magazines that had been initialled by all his staff. I can remember to this day the exhilaration I felt on reading "new thoughts" about business ethics, the moral foundations for capitalism, and the concepts of free markets and individual responsibility – ideas that had never before entered my consciousness.

These ideas influenced my thinking greatly. Later when I was studying at the Kalgoorlie School of Mines, I became the Editor of the *School of Mines Magazine* and would often publish articles inspired by the ideas I had learned from those crumpled pages of *The Freeman*. However, Kalgoorlie, a mining town, back then was pretty much controlled by the unions. My "radical" content did not go down very well in the general community and I found myself in deep water trying to defend my published positions.

In desperation I wrote to Mr Leonard E. Read, the President of the Foundation for Economic Education (publisher of *The Freeman*) for help, and to let them know that their ideas were getting me into trouble! Mr Read responded with encouragement and sent me regular copies of *The Freeman*.

In his reply he suggested that the reason I was having so much trouble with my Kalgoorlie audience may have been because I hadn't spent enough time understanding my own position. He made it clear that principles of liberty and freedom started way back with the musings of Greek philosopher Aristotle having been polished up over the years and that there was much for me to learn. The job of life-long learning never ends, as Leonard was at pains to teach me, in what became a series of thoughtful letters.

Over the years I wrote some of my own articles and submitted them to the editor of *The Freeman*, but I was never published, and I couldn't work out why.

After seeing all my rejected submissions, he must have taken pity on me, as in one letter he very politely gave me some useful advice. He suggested that my writing may have been a little "pushy" then said, "You only have a licence to change yourself, not others. All you can do is bring an idea to the threshold of someone's consciousness, and then it is up to them to accept it or reject that idea after due consideration. If they then accept that idea, it will be with them for life."

The first letter from Leonard was the start of a lifelong friendship and mentorship, and he has had many occasions to advise me over the years. Another time he said to me, "As one acquires an awareness of how little one knows, humility replaces arrogance; this tends to improve a person's nature and sense of humour." Leonard's quiet reasoning certainly had an effect on my own approach and communication style, helping me to improve my writing, and get published in so many places.

So, what stood out for me about Leonard Read's leadership style? As well as fully understanding the philosophy and principles behind advocacy for free markets and personal responsibility, he realised there had to be a strategy in place to share those ideas in such a way that people were more receptive to them. Leonard felt that we all only have a licence to change ourselves, and in that way, we become a beacon. If we shine brightly enough others will see the light and become illuminated by new ideas.

Of course, Leonard had remembered how I first stumbled on those pages from The Freeman in my father's crates of Timken's roller bearings and one day in 1982 he invited me to tell this story to a group of his directors and staff in New York. I was hesitant at first thinking it was a fairly boring story, but he assured me that if I started the story, he would finish it. Leonard's colleagues enjoyed hearing about me opening the old crates and finding the crumpled pages that had already done the rounds among the executives of Timken's before being recycled as packing material.

Leonard completed my story by reiterating his own saying – "ideas have consequences". Their actions in publishing *The Freeman* resulted in a young man on the other side of the world becoming interested in the philosophy of freedom, eventually leading to the establishment of the Mannkal Economic Education Foundation, based as it is on Leonard's

PACKING PAPER REVELATIONS

ABOVE: Leonard E. Read in his Foundation for Economic Education (FEE) office, explains some of the finer points of the free market to his Australian colleague Ron Manners, New York, 1982.

Left: FEE's monthly magazine The Freeman has always had a wide circle of readers.

own FEE. He concluded by saying, "Gentlemen, our ideas had more consequences that we had ever dreamt of."
I had no idea back in my teenage years when I first started reading those crumpled pages of *The Freeman*, that 69 years later after my philosophical journey began, I would be appointed to the Board of the Mont Pelerin Society, an organisation that has been central to the international free market movement for 75 years. Now, 69 years to graduate to the Board may seem like a lengthy career path, but if you asked me, I would say that I exceeded my expectations, and all thanks to Leonard Read's leadership and his influence on my life.

Leonard took the time to write me a letter of advice and encouragement all those years ago, when he could see that I was struggling with the ideas espoused in the pages of The Freeman and how best to promote them. In this way he was leading by example and by taking time out of his day to share his knowledge with me, he revealed that each one of us has the capacity to do the same. Leonard's leadership style therefore was in my estimation 50 percent philosophy and 50 percent strategy. He understood that it is not enough to just have the knowledge, we must all understand what we can do with it and how we can effectively impart it to others.

WHAT DOES THE CAUSE OF LIBERTY NEED MOST?

Leonard E. Read, the founder of FEE, insisted that what liberty needs most is not better politics, propaganda, or marketing, but better thought leadership. What libertarians face, Read wrote, is not a "political action" problem, a "mass reformation problem," or a "selling problem," but a "leadership problem." *https://fee.org/articles/habits-of-effective-libertarians/*

ABOVE: John Hospers in London, 1984.

Left: John Hospers and Jenny Manners visiting the 'slab' from the Berlin Wall at the Reagan Presidential Library, 2004.

Below : Plaque – Berlin Wall.

THE UNSPEAKABLY 'EVIL' TEXTBOOK PROFESSOR JOHN HOSPERS

I've written elsewhere about the gentle influence Professor John Hospers had on me. In my previous books and more recently in a guest chapter for the recent publication of *Libertarianism: John Hospers, the Libertarian Party's 50th Anniversary, and Beyond* – https://www.mannwest.com/books/libertarianism/ (The publishers of this book 'rounded up' a collection of former students of John Hospers and gave each of us a chapter to write.) It may seem as though I have talked often about Professor Hospers, but to me his contribution has been significant.

Professor Hospers' influence found me very early on when his book *An Introduction to Philosophical Analysis* was the textbook of a philosophy unit in which I enrolled at the University of Western Australia in 1961. I go into the reasons for my initial interest in philosophy elsewhere, and if you have read about it, you will know that *Playboy* magazine and Hugh Hefner's philosophical editorials played no small part. Yes, I read *Playboy* for the articles!

I enjoyed the university course immensely, in particular, the way Hospers' mind worked. In *An Introduction to Philosophical Analysis*, he advocated strongly for the concept of personal responsibility which resonated deeply with me. It came as a shock to me then, when one day in a barber shop, I read an article in *Pix* magazine that described an 'unspeakably evil' book. It didn't take long for me to realise that the book in question was the very same Hospers textbook that so impressed me during my course at university.

Later that night, worried that there was something in the book I had missed, I skimmed through it again looking for the 'evil' that was so obvious to the author of that article, but to no avail. What that author had thought of as 'evil' were the exact things that I had admired when reading the book – an elevation of 'heroic self-responsibility'. Was there an error in my understanding?

I took it upon myself then to write to Professor Hospers to seek clarity and to my surprise he responded. He pointed out to me that any academic who puts their views forward was often subject to attacks such as these. Little did I know at the time, this correspondence marked the beginning of a lifelong friendship which lasted from when I wrote that letter in 1961 all the way to his death in 2011 at the age of 93.

Hospers is well-known in philosophical circles for his work in aesthetics, in particular his 1982 book *Understanding the Arts*. He also authored two textbooks, the aforementioned An Introduction to Philosophical Analysis first published in 1953, and *Human Conduct: Problems of Ethics* published in 1995. After becoming closely acquainted with Ayn Rand in New York, Hospers' interest in libertarianism became manifest in the volume *Libertarianism: A Political Philosophy for Tomorrow* published in 1971.

On the basis of that book, and his stature as a philosopher, the US Libertarian Party ran Hospers as their first Presidential Candidate in 1972. Although he was only on the ballot in Colorado and Washington, he campaigned widely across the nation in the cities and on college campuses. Although he and his running mate received only 3,971 votes, they did achieve one electoral college vote and Hospers' campaign rallied many libertarians to the Libertarian Party. Soon after his foray into politics, Hospers returned to what he loved most: academia and teaching.

In 1982 I was travelling home to Australia from New York via Los Angeles where I was to spend a day and a night. This would be an ideal opportunity for me to catch up with John as he was at the time the Director of the School of Philosophy at the University of Southern California. We made plans to meet for dinner and I was eagerly looking forward to mulling over various questions of philosophy with him in person.

Unfortunately, a complication with the airline meant that my flights were changed, and I would have only four hours at the airport instead of an overnight layover. I rang John from New York to let him know and explained that we would have to settle for a phone call, and as I had only four questions for him, we could manage that as a consolation.

I clearly recall John's response which was to immediately ask me if I did indeed have four hours to spare at the airport. When I confirmed that was so, he replied, "Ron, you only have four questions for me, but I have twenty questions for you so I will come to the airport, and we can sit quietly for four hours."

Our four-hour meeting at the Los Angeles airport 1982.

So that is what we did, while consuming several drinks! John's twenty questions all had something to do with how I had managed to come to the same conclusions as he, on a range of issues but all from a completely different direction. John knew that I had been put out of business numerous times by my refusal to join the cosy cartels of occupational licensing, and because he had been writing about the threats of unrestrained government, I suspect he viewed me as a fresh specimen and a worthy subject for his study.

In 1984, I was involved with organising the Libertarian International 2nd World Convention in London. We invited Hospers as our keynote speaker where he compared George Orwell's novel 1984 to 1776, the year of the American Revolution, and spoke on several topics including dystopia, technology, and failure of global communism. It was another opportunity for me to spend time with John in person and exchange our philosophical views.

Later, in 1996 I recall my wife Jenny and I having a very long dinner with John in Los Angeles. At the time he was struggling with some health issues and was greatly concerned about custodial care of his considerable archive of papers and correspondence. His most pressing concern was for the detailed advice on constitutions and government structures he had been providing to several new-nation projects. I had been actively involved in one of these projects with him, the saga of New Hebrides that resulted in the independence of Vanuatu, and so I was intimately aware of the value of the advice he offered. It's my sincere hope that these writings of Hospers' were suitably conserved.

The last time I met John in person was in 2004 when he spent a full day with me and Jenny, acting as our personal tour guide when we visited the Ronald Reagan Presidential Library and Museum in California. If you have not visited the Ronald Reagan Library before you may be unaware that it is financed entirely though private donations, as are most presidential libraries in the United States, except for the underground vault that stores the official Presidential papers.

On the day, John proved to be the most magnificent tour guide. After visiting all the public areas, we then moved down to the underground vault, but I was disappointed to learn that Presidential papers are under secure guard and we were informed that we would not be permitted to enter the vault.

This problem was quickly resolved, however, when I proudly announced that John Hospers was a former Presidential Candidate. From that moment we were treated as V.I.P.s and were allocated a special research guide who showed us every imaginable document including Reagan's hand-written amendments to speech-writer's documents, that transformed them into the very personally focused speeches for which he was so noted.

The Hospers' book I studied at university, *An Introduction to Philosophical Analysis*, has influenced me enormously, and throughout my life I have often had reason to refer back to it. I clearly remember one occasion during a period of my life when I was managing a hotel in Bali. The local staff used to laugh at Australians when from time to time they described the food served as 'beautiful'. They explained to me that in Indonesian, the word for 'beautiful' is used to describe many things, but never food.

This led me to recall Hospers discussing the meaning of the word beautiful. He said that "We are generally inclined to speak of objects as 'beautiful' when they arouse in us aesthetic experiences." Thus, I believe he would have approved of the use of the word to describe delicious food. Professor Hospers never did sit back on his laurels. He always endeavoured to refine his thinking, and to impart his ideas to others as clearly as could be managed. The textbook which so strongly influenced me, was revised three times, the fourth and final edition reduced from 532 pages down to 282 which, to me, makes it abundantly clear that over time Hospers was able to articulate his ideas more clearly.

Never one for pretence, John Hospers made it clear in his own writings that he wanted to be remembered as a great teacher. He rightly realised that universities in general do not value an ability to teach in their lecturers and professors, and instead the focus is on whether they are getting published in niche journals. In his own words:

I am mostly known as a writer of philosophy. But I always desired to be remembered as a great teacher. Universities, however, consider only a teacher's scholarly works and not their teaching ability. I want to be remembered as a philosophical instructor who could clarify questions and present good ideas clearly, avoiding vagueness and confusion in the presentation of ideas. That is probably my main legacy as a teacher and many of my students have come to remember me in just that way.

It is clear that Professor John Hospers' leadership style was entirely driven by philosophy, and what a successful leader and teacher he was. His aim to was make clear his thoughts and share them with others through his writing and teaching, and yet although he did not focus on any strategic action, his influence has been and continues to be enormous, reinforcing my belief that good ideas flow upward, rather than sink downward. Hospers was unencumbered by strategy.

"We are the intellectual spearheads of the coming renaissance of liberty. Just as the intellectual influence of the Fabians propelled Britain into socialism a century ago, so the intellectual influence of libertarians can turn Britain, and indeed the world, back to individual liberty because now the soil has been prepared.

The consequences of socialism in practise are increasingly

plain for anyone with eyes to see. "It's essence of man" said Aristotle, "to make decisions. His own decisions, not those made for him by others." To implement this simple but profound truth and to apply it over and over again, in its countless manifestations in our individual and social lives; that is our libertarian mission. Surely, it's the noblest of goals, and I see no good reason why we should not be able to achieve it."

That was a typical John Hospers call to action and a fitting way to conclude my commemoration of this great teacher. *Conclusion to my chapter in 'Libertarianism: John Hospers' – https://www.mannwest.com/books/libertarianism/*

Some members of the "Z group" with hosts planning their strategies for the following day. Left to right: S. (Wanga) Waqanivavalagi [Fiji]; Host; Rodney Gibson [Aust.]; Neil Cole (host); Peter Gavai [India]; Ron Manners [Aust.].

> "The objective is for the members to look,
> listen and learn in the hope that the process will help them
> to improve the quality of their decision making
> when they reach the peak of their occupations."
>
> HRH The Duke of Edinburgh

In May 2006 (38 years later) a proud father enters Buckingham Palace with his daughter, Sarah Basden (nee Manners), who was representing Rio Tinto plc. The occasion was the 50th Anniversary Celebration of the Commonwealth Leadership Development Conferences – https://www.cscglobalalumni.org/

NO PHILOSOPHER PRINCE

HRH Prince Philip, The Duke of Edinburgh

In stark contrast to John Hospers is Prince Philip. Instead of being driven by a deep interest in philosophy and economics, Prince Philip instead approached his endeavours with practicality of mind and a firm commitment to achieving outcomes. 100% strategy.

In 1954 Prince Philip travelled to Canada where he observed a number of single industry "company towns" facing challenges in establishing democratic means by which the management and workers could live together as a community outside of the workplace. This inspired him to establish the Commonwealth Study Conference. In his own words "the purpose of the conference was to look into the tensions, problems and opportunities created by the dichotomy between industrial enterprise and community development."

The first Commonwealth Study Conference, "an extraordinary experiment" was held in Oxford, UK in 1956. Philip invited participants from diverse sectors of society including government representatives, non-governmental organisations, trade unions and businesspeople from all the Commonwealth countries with a view bringing together groups of people who are at times antagonistic towards each other in the spirit of collaboration. Truly an ambitious project. In his own words, "The objective was for members to look, listen and learn in the hope that the process will help them to improve the quality of their decision-making when they reach the peaks of their occupations."

It would be easy to believe that not much could be achieved by bringing such diverse groups together to collaborate, however, since 1956 there have been ten separate Commonwealth Study Conferences hosted in Canada, Australia, New Zealand, India, Malaysia, and the United Kingdom attended by an average of 300 participants each time. A success by any measure.

So how did Prince Philip pull it off?

I was fortunate enough to attend a number of Commonwealth Study Conferences first of which was in Australia. In 1968 I was accepted to attend what was then known as the "Duke of Edinburgh Study Conference" against some stiff competition. When I later met one of the selection panel members (Senator Dorothy Tangney) I asked if she could remember why I was chosen and she recalled that at the time, I stood out because I had solved a salinity problem on our Esperance (south coast) farm by planting

Pucinellia – the first planting in Australia. It was the view of the selection panel that such problem solving should be encouraged. I mention this to highlight to that we can never know where our curiosity can lead us! (I had researched the success of this salt-eating plant in Turkey, so imported Australia's first Pucinellia from Turkey, with spectacular results. (*Pucinellia was my one success during my 40 years of farming.*) https://www.mannwest.com/forty-years-of-farming/

As a consequence of being accepted to join the Conference, I was privileged to meet the man himself. My first observation of Prince Philip was that he did not seek to impose any economic philosophy on his guests. To do so would have been viewed as "taking sides" with one sector against another. Bear in mind that representatives from industry, trade unions and government were being effectively "locked up" together for a period of three weeks. After this period of intense collaborative effort, participants from the different sectors came to an understanding of each other realising that they each had a common goal which could be boiled down into "just getting on with it" as Prince Philip himself used to say.

To encourage a free exchange of ideas, he taught us that when debating or negotiating, or even just getting to know somebody, if you want to get a person's real opinion you will likely need to ask them the same question more than once. His view was that the first time you ask a question, a person may not answer you as they may think you are simply being polite.

The second time the question is asked, a person may take the questioner a little more seriously and give a partial answer. Only on the third time will the person realise they are being taken seriously and will be more likely to fully open up and give you their real opinion.

"Curious people ask questions. Successful people get answers."

Prince Philip encouraged attendees at the Conference to think and speak for themselves, rather than seeing themselves as just a spokesperson for their organisation. He hoped this would avert the pitfalls of "group thinking". He also had a special message for the Australian participants, and that was to "get over" our perceived distrust of excellence. He wanted us all to be unafraid to excel and to be the best people we could be.

Prince Philip had a personal style that I admired. The following year, in 1969, a follow-up conference was held which I also attended. On the stroke of 10am, just as the conference was due to open, almost out of nowhere a helicopter landed near the front steps of Keele University (Stoke-on-Trent UK), and out leapt Prince Philip, still buttoning up his jacket as he greeted us all. He had piloted himself to the conference, and as always, punctual.

In public life, Prince Philip was known for his "zingers"

– his often brutally honest one-liners. But he also spoke with deep wisdom, such as in the below letter penned to the Institute of Economic Affairs in 1983:

Fashion is not restricted to clothes, and when ideas become fashionable, they are just as resistant to objective criticism as the length of skirts. That is why all economic ideas need to be freely discussed judged against the facts of real life. I hope that "Economic Affairs" will help all its readers to sift the rational from the wishful and the practical from the fashionable.

Unlike Professor John Hospers, Prince Philip espoused no political philosophy, absolutely none, but this was the key to his success. If he had any philosophical input into his Commonwealth Study Conferences, then he would have had arguments between the trade unions, business, and the government people. Instead, Prince Philip's sincere hope was that the Commonwealth Study Conferences would facilitate life-long bonds being formed between traditionally the "warring parties" such that the benefits would become obvious during subsequent years and help to build a better Commonwealth.

I can personally attest to the success of Prince Philip's endeavour and his pragmatic approach through his influence on me in developing the Mannkal Economic Education Foundation. In 1968, at age 32, I was thrust into his world when I attended my first Commonwealth Study

Conference where I saw for myself his strong focus on training and action, leading me to formulate the two-fold approach that we would develop at Mannkal 29 years later in 1997. Our focus on economic education was inspired by Leonard Read and the Foundation for Economic Education, but our "how" has been greatly inspired by Prince Philip's focus on strategy.

How do I know that Prince Philip's study conference was a life changing experience for me? I will never forget the feeling of complete emptiness on my return to my normal life. I had no one to share my experiences with. My colleagues and friends had stood still, as though in a Time Machine during my absence, and could not comprehend that I was no longer the earlier Ron. This has enabled me to empathise with others returning from similar experiences. Perhaps by a factor of 10, this could be those returning from war service – I have many friends who have returned from their Vietnam War experience and felt a similar feeling of 'complete remoteness'.

If our Scholars experience the same feeling, then I feel that our challenge has been successful.

Do they share this feeling of 'emotional disequilibrium'? I sense that this is the case each time I observe our returned students exchanging stories with one another. "If you haven't been there, you don't understand!"

In discussion with HRH Prince Philip – Canberra.

For more details including four YouTube presentations from former Study Conference participants:-

https://www.mannwest.com/hrh-prince-philip-ideas-have-consequences/

THE IMPATIENT LIBERTARIAN

THE STORY OF INFLATION AND HOW HAYEK GOT CONTROL OF THE BEAST.

An outstanding young bull was purchased by Mont Pelerin Society member, Ron Kitching, Principal of North Queensland's leading Brahman Stud. After residing on the property for 12 months, it was noticed that the bull would not stop growing and finally topped 3,000 pounds. Mr Kitching nicknamed him 'Inflation' because he would not stop growing.

On his 1976 lecture tour Professor F.A. Hayek had a four-day holiday on the property. On being introduced to 'Inflation' the professor agreed that he was indeed a formidable proposition to tackle. However, he drew from his experience in handling animals, which was considerable from his days in the Austrian Army.

"My experience with inflation", said Hayek, "Is that you must act quickly and boldly if you are to arrest it." He thus strode over and without further ado, very quickly 'had Inflation by the balls.'

KNOWLEDGE? NOT A PROBLEM

Professor F.A. Hayek

My first direct contact with my favourite economist Friedrich Hayek was in 1976 when my friend Ron Kitching suggested I pitch in to help bring Hayek to Australia. A few of us, including Viv Forbes, Roger Randerson and Kitching contributed some cash and managed to entice Hayek to our shores.

Hayek, accompanied by his wife, spent five weeks in Australia. While here he travelled the east coast from Cairns in Queensland all the way down to Melbourne and across to Adelaide. Roger Randerson, a former student of Hayek's at the London School of Economics, organised his tour which resulted in over 60 meetings, appointments and lectures, including an appearance on the ABC's *Monday Conference* – *https://bit.ly/49EqWMP* which was a similar program to today's *Q&A*. Full details of his tour have been well documented by Rafe Champion in his chapter "Hayek in Australia, 1976" which appears in *Hayek: a Collective Bibliography* (2015).

Sadly, the classical liberalism and libertarian movement was not well organised in Australia at the time of his visit, so it is difficult to fully assess the impact of Hayek's visit to our shores. Apart from a brief stir after his appearance on *Monday Conference*, the media was virtually silent regarding his visit and not one of the four major newspapers at the time mentioned it, despite reporting on Milton Friedman's Nobel Prize which was awarded while Hayek was still on tour. Maybe ignorance is to blame.

Fortunately, three of Hayek's Australian lectures were captured and published by The Centre for Independent Studies (as *Occasional Papers #2*) – it quickly became a 'collector's item'.

After exchanging letters with Hayek, in 1997, I had the pleasure of meeting with him a few times after that, including Hong Kong in 1978, Berlin in 1982 and Tokyo in 1988 (after attending 24 Mont Pelerin meetings, I've been asked to assemble a photo album, to capture many of the true characters involved).

I valued these occasions immensely. Hayek made it clear to me that he also valued spending time with business people and non-academics as he felt that we were "closer to reality". As well as that he was keen to know that his ideas were being sufficiently expressed in layman's terms such that we 'ordinary folk' we able to understand and apply them.

One time during our conversation (Berlin 1982) I was

having some difficulty in keeping up with his train of thought. I implored him to slow down telling him "I'm not an economist!" He responded by saying "I'm glad you're not an economist. We economists simply dream our ideas and think our thoughts, but businesspeople like you go out and fire the bullets!" His view was that entrepreneurs and businesspeople enjoy volatility as they know, rightly, that it is from volatility new opportunities arise. So, he also appreciated our ability to put his ideas into action.

Hayek's life-long interest in economics was spawned by his desire to improve social conditions, particularly in post-WWI Vienna. He was heavily influenced by Ludwig von Mises' 1922 book *Die Gemeinwirtshaft (Socialism)* and claimed that "to none of us, who read the book… the world was ever the same again". Over many years he sparred with Keynes, and despite decline in the popularity of Austrian economics, in 1974 Hayek received the Nobel Memorial Prize in Economic Sciences. This saw a resurgence of interest in the Austrian school meaning that a whole new generation of people was exposed to his writings.

During WWII Hayek offered his services to the British Ministry of Information to assist them with 'propaganda aimed at German-speaking countries that would demonstrate the similarity between the principles of liberty espoused by England and France and those of German poets and intellectuals of the past'. Sadly, his offer of help was declined. Instead, he continued to work on a project dubbed "The Abuse of Reason", which included several historical chapters. Eventually his focus narrowed to the last section of his planned book, which he transformed into a shorter political tract that resulted in Hayek's arguably most popular book *The Road to Serfdom*.

It is not known exactly what motivated Hayek to shift his focus at this time, but some have speculated that while an Allied loss in Europe would have been catastrophic, Hayek was fearful that a victory would result in socialists wanting to continue into peacetime the economic controls that were necessary during the war, writing "wisdom in the management of our economic affairs will be even more important than before and that the fate of our civilisation will ultimately depend on how we solve the economic problems we shall then face." Thankfully he took the time to anticipate this eventual outcome and work towards combatting these ideas.

In *The Road to Serfdom* Hayek challenged what most economists at the time believed -that for an economy to work well, it needed centralised control and management. Even though it is a common belief that an economy needs some form of political intervention in the market, it is acknowledged by most people that central planning is not inevitable, and that competition in the marketplace plays an important role. This shift in general perception is attributed

Hanging proudly in Mannkal Foundation's office is this framed photo taken by the author in Berlin, 1982.

The building is called Hayek-on-Hood, in Hood Street, Subiaco, Perth, Western Australia.

to the impact of *The Road to Serfdom*.

Although originally rejected by three US publishing houses, the book was eventually published by the University of Chicago Press, selling out its first run within ten days, and today more that 2 million copies have been sold[1]. Even Hayek's economic adversary John Maynard Keynes praised it saying, "Morally and philosophically I find myself in agreement with virtually the whole of it, and not only in agreement with it, but a deeply moved agreement." If only he had agreed with Hayek more often!

It turns out that after publication, Hayek become something of a star in the world of economics, touring the United States for five weeks in 1945. One event at the Town Hall Club in New York attracted a crowd of over

---

[1] "The Publication History of The Road to Serfdom", excerpted from Bruce Caldwell's introduction to *The Road to Serfdom: Text and Documents – The Definitive Edition* by F. A. Hayek

Jenny Manners being shown F.A. Hayek's original manual typewriter on which he wrote his books and correspondence. Pictured with the late Dr. Lawrence Hayek (son of F.A. Hayek) – London 2002.

A visit to the Vienna gravesite of F.A. Hayek. From left: Jenny Manners, Michael Checkan, Prof. Mark Skousen, author – 2002.

Bronze bust of F.A. Hayek that was presented to the Kremlin in Russia by Mr Ed Crane, President of the CATO Institute – September 1990.

The Hayek bust, by a Miami Sculptor was organized by George Koether and Ron Manners with a 'twin' produced for Mannkal's office.

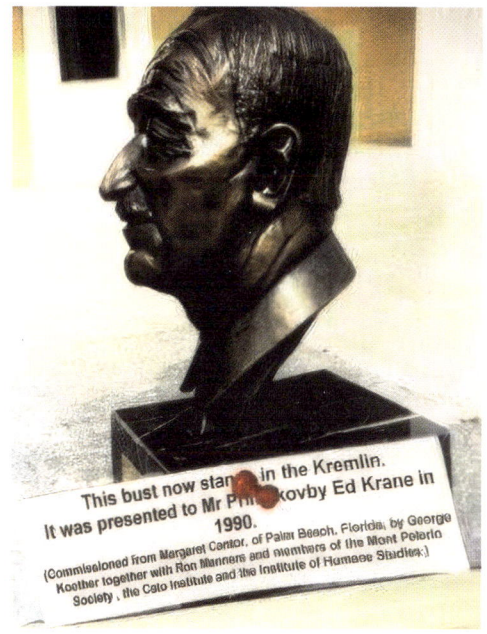

February 9th, 1977

Dear Mr. Manners, thank you for your kind letter of the 11th of last month which, because of my absence from here, has only just reached me. It was pleasant to hear from you after missing you in Australia.

I have so far seen little effect of my Denationalization of Currency beyond a few kind but rather puzzlied reviews in newspapers and weekly journals. The people seem to find it difficult to believe that I meant it seriously.

Please note that from the end of this month my address will be
        Urachstrasse 27
        D-78 FREIBURG i.Brg.
        West Germany.

                Sincerely,

                F.A.Hayek

The patient professor replied to my many questions.

3,000 people. A newspaper interview revealed that Hayek was "at first a bit puzzled and even alarmed when I found that a book written in no party spirit... should have been so exclusively welcomed by one party and so thoroughly excoriated by the other." He was concerned that his ideas may be used by businesses in favour of trade tariffs to argue against government intervention on one hand while ignoring his support for free trade for everyone and lobbying for more intervention in the market. Another reason he had plenty of time for businesspeople – he wanted to make sure we really understood his message.

What struck me about Hayek's leadership style during our acquaintance was his ability to give apt advice and his willingness to engage with people from many walks of life. Although he was himself an academic, he wanted his ideas and economic insights to be understood by us all, and most importantly, he wanted to see them implemented. Strategy, then, was important to him. It was always Hayek's firm belief that state control of economic life cannot enhance human wellbeing and will result in misery and poverty, and he dedicated his life to promoting this thesis.

Hundreds of people wrote to Hayek just to get guidance on what they should be doing to be more effective.

How to rate Hayek with respect to Ideas and Strategy?

His mind was certainly travelling at top speed with abundant ideas that he put to good use in 'manufacturing intellectual bullets'.

Unlike many academics he realised that this is not enough. I'd say that 25% of his focus was on recruiting 'intellectual soldiers'. One such person was Sir Anthony Fisher.

Sir Antony Fisher who was to become so influential in the freedom movement, and the fifth leader to whom I pay tribute in this volume.

Hayek's remarkable Nobel lecture – *https://fee.org/articles/remembering-hayek-s-remarkable-nobel-lecture/*

"My Crowning Moment", was receiving the Sir Antony Fisher Lifetime Achievement Award for 2020. Although presented via Zoom (due to Australia's Covid lockdown), a large gathering was assembled in New York for a formal dinner. In Perth we celebrated with a bacon and egg breakfast, including champagne.

THE TRIUMPH OF THE EGG SMUGGLER

Sir Antony Fisher AFC

After returning home from his stint as a war-time fighter pilot hero in WWII, Fisher saw that England was in terrible shape. He had read Hayek's condensed version of *The Road to Serfdom* and wanted to go into politics, but first he organised to meet with Hayek at the London School of Economics. Hayek advised him not to go into politics as "you will just become like all the other politicians and in the end the results will not be what your goals are. Instead go and start a Think Tank, get people together like yourself. Generate a lot of ideas. Always remember politicians are not leaders, they are followers. You must get the public to start accepting these ideas, then the politicians will follow those ideas because they think there are votes in it."

Hayek then suggested to Fisher that he not proceed with that plan immediately but make some money first, because you cannot achieve anything unless you have enough money to finance it. So, Fisher went into the chicken business and ultimately became the biggest chicken farmer in England forming the company Buxted Chickens which in 1964 was producing 500,000 chickens a week.

On his chicken journey Fisher went to America where he discovered the chickens were a different breed - bigger and better with twice as much meat on them. The breed that existed in England was scrawny in comparison because they were all controlled by government boards and there was no competition.

Fisher then tried to get permission to bring back some of these chickens to breed in England, but his request was denied by the Egg Marketing Board. So a week or two before Easter, Fisher went to America, got half a suitcase of fertilised eggs, wrapped them all up so that they looked like Easter eggs, brought them back in his bag, got them through Customs and started breeding the super chickens, becoming the biggest chicken producer in the United Kingdom. Then, sold the company and with that capital he established the Institute of Economic Affairs (IEA) and then the Manhattan Institute and then the Pacific Institute. He was populating the world with Think Tanks including the Atlas Network which is widely influential today by providing inspiration to over 500 independent partner Think Tanks world-wide.

What a story! We can see that Sir Antony Fisher's leadership style was at least seventy five percent strategy, all stemming from Hayek's astute advice. The power of a single person giving the right advice is immeasurable.

https://www.mannwest.com/sir-antony-fisher-from-law-breaker-to-knighthood/

https://www.youtube.com/watch?v=Xeb6GULHao0

https://www.mannwest.com/2020-the-year-of-the-awards/

ALL FIVE – ALL DIFFERENT. ANY CONSISTENT CHARACTERISTICS? HEROIC HUMILITY.

What have I learned from examining the 'style' and methods followed by my selected five influences?

Their styles may differ, but their results and influence were all admirable.

If their 'styles' differ, what did they have in common?

- Their focus, their clarity of purpose, all bordering on the 'heroic'. No sign of fatigue. Never any last gasp, "Well, I have finished my task!"

- No self-aggrandisement, no big 'name in lights' extravaganzas. 'Humility' almost taken to extreme (with humility never confused with timidity). Could we describe their mutual shared style as being one of 'Heroic Humility'? Perhaps those two words embody the life-work of all five?

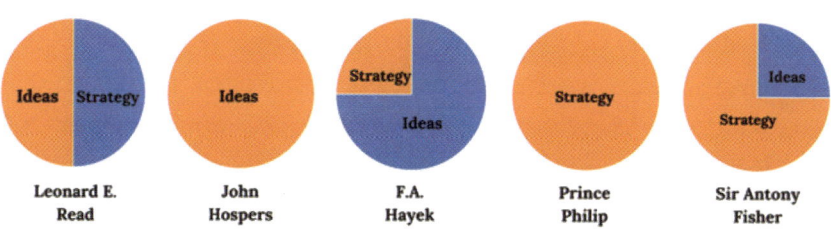

PART 2

LIFE: ONE ACCIDENT AFTER ANOTHER! – DEVELOPING AN ART FORM?

So far, I have introduced you to five people who have created my impatience and demonstrated how my life has been a series of accidents, one after another.

I came across the earlier mentioned five figures in my life, all by accident.

LEONARD E READ

This was completely accidental just by opening large packing boxes and smoothing out the crumpled packing material. Curiosity led me to read the contents of these crumpled pages from *The Freeman magazine*.

PROFESSOR JOHN HOSPERS

If I had not been reading Hugh Hefner's introductory *Playboy Philosophy* in the magazine that he published (*Playboy*) I would never have been curious enough to proceed in signing up for Philosophy 1 at the University of Western Australia.

HRH PRINCE PHILIP – DUKE OF EDINBURGH

If I had not been a member of the Jaycees (Junior Chamber) at an early age I would not have ever met Phillip Lynch – *https://en.wikipedia.org/wiki/Phillip_Lynch* – the then National President of the Jaycees[2]. It was his answer to my question to him, "What is the single most influential event in your life that has led to your success?" His answer was, without doubt and any hesitation, "I was fortunate in being selected for the Duke of Edinburgh Study Conference and if you ever get the opportunity to apply let me tell you, "just do it."

The second accident leading me to this opportunity was a surprise breakfast meeting… see[3]

F.A. HAYEK

If my friend, Ronald Kitching, had not been a little short on for 'cash', on the day, he may not have approached me for some financial assistance to further his ambition to have Hayek visit Australia.

I'm sure without this personal involvement I never would have developed a long-standing friendship with F.A. Hayek.

ANTONY FISHER

All these 'accidents' helped me later to recognize the 'road

---

[2] I met Phillip Lynch in 1966. He was Managing Director of Management Consultants Manpower (Australia) Pty Ltd, later that year he entered parliament. Knighted in Dec. 1980 and died at age 50 in 1984. His amazing life was covered in Lynched authored by Brian Buckley.

[3] "Avoiding a Misplaced Perception of One's own Importance" https://www.mannwest.com/avoiding-the-misplaced-perception-of-ones-own-importance/ This is the second 'accident' involving this opportunity.

taken' by Antony Fisher and seek him out. The rest, simply fell into place from there.

My 'track record' for attracting accidents has followed me and several of my major business accidents became a successful book called *Heroic Misadventures* – *https://www.mannwest.com/books/heroic-misadventures/*

Most of the time I have managed to turn these accidents into opportunities. Isn't that what life is all about?

May I now ask...

"Could attracting accidental events be developed into an art form?"

> *"Problems are only opportunities in work clothes."*
>
> Henry J. Kaiser

The last photo taken of grandfather 'PomPom' Stevens. Upon his death, I was sent to Esperance 'to look after my grandmother for that year', until my parents arranged a home for her in Kalgoorlie. Pictured here with my grandparents, my mother Nancy and younger sister Frances.

POM POM'S CLARINET

Why on earth was I sitting against a wall playing a clarinet with a group of Aboriginal People in Laverton (Central Western Australia), on a fine sunny day in 1962?

Bear with me and I will explain the sequence of accidental events.

It all started when I was six years old. I grew up in Kalgoorlie. Four hours south, by car, is Esperance, where one set of my grandparents lived. That grandfather was known as "Pom Pom" Stevens and nobody seemed to know his first name. He was called Pom Pom because he was a prospector, a clarinet player, a choir master and all the time he walked around the house he would be humming, "pom, pom, pom".

My recollection was of an imposing '7-foot-tall' bearded man. The beard, was stained from chewing tobacco. He was something of an artist at chewing tobacco. He and my grandmother lived in a one-room house in Esperance, with a couple of small bedrooms tucked on the side. In each corner of the main room was a kerosine tin cut in

Appreciative audience at Laverton, Western Australia, 1962.

half, with the sides turned down, full of sand. If Pom Pom walked into the room from one corner, he would fire his spittle from the chewed tobacco into the diagonally opposite sand pit spittoon and never miss. At age six this impressed me greatly.

What might seem strange today is that Pom Pom never spoke to me. Back in those days grandchildren were just something to be tolerated and grandparents did not need to know their names and in general saw no need to speak to them. That was just the way it was back mid-last century. I respected his desire to detest me, and I responded with admiration.

One night Pom Pom came home after 11.00 pm, and I heard a disturbance in this one large room. Curiosity got the better of me and I snuck out of bed to investigate just what was going on. I soon discovered. He arrived home from the pub with four large brown paper parcels under his arm and he opened them up on the kitchen table. They were strings of sausages. Remember, he did not know I was sitting in the corner watching as I was not on his radar at all.

Strangely enough he proceeded to take down all the pictures around the room, leaving all the bare nails where he hung the strings of sausages. I suspected he may have had a couple of drinks. He then went up to the mantlepiece where he had an Edison phonograph with a big horn on it and cylindrical records. He cranked it up and I heard some magnificent J.P. Sousa marches among others.[4] He then pulled out his clarinet, stood up on a chair, put the clarinet down in the bell and played the most amazing music.

To me in that moment it was just fabulous. I was captured by the connection between my grandfather and his instrument. It clearly meant so much to him. After playing each piece he turned around, still standing on the chair, bowed at all the sausages and, in the true spirit of that moment, I imagined the sausages cheering in return.

That was my early memory of my grandfather. Two years later, he died, and the families all headed down to Esperance. Back in those days there was no refrigeration, and they just left Pom Pom's deceased body in his bed until

---

[4] Much later I identified two of the marches he played that night: Blaze Away by Abe Holzman and Under the Double Eagle by J. F. Wallace.

the various families arrived (about 3-4 days later). It was then that I heard his family discussing what they were going to do with his clarinet. The plan was to put it in his coffin and bury it with him because, they too, realised how much it meant to him.

"Bugger that", thought my 8-year-old self, believing that old Pom Pom would have felt there to be much life left in his old clarinet. So, I snuck into the bedroom and "nicked" it. Come the morning of the funeral, the family was running around asking "where is Pom Pom's clarinet?" When they could not locate it, they abandoned that plan and fastened down the lid to the coffin. I hid that clarinet for a few years, and later, when I "confessed", my mother and father forgave me with a smile.

I took no immediate steps to play that clarinet myself. I was then very much involved with playing the piano and making great progress, winning a few trophies along the way. However, a few years later when I was seventeen, I was in an accident. I was driving a car with my parents as passengers, returning from Esperance to Kalgoorlie. There was a truck coming in the opposite direction, at night, and there was some oversized machinery on the back of the truck which tore out the side of our car. As I was the driver, it took my arm along with it.

The next thing I knew I was in hospital, under sedation, sitting in a wheelchair and I heard my father arguing with the doctor, Alan Webster. Dr Webster said, "Charlie, I'm going to cut Ron's arm off just here." He had the equivalent of a Texta (Sharpie) and as he was speaking, he was marking a line on my arm. He said to my father, "It's too far gone, and we will never save it." I vividly remember my father's reply, "Alan you might be a very good friend of mine and that might be very good advice, but I'm going to take Ron to Perth tomorrow and seek a second opinion." That action resulted in my arm being saved and I learned an early lesson. You can get advice from the experts, but it is best sometimes to ignore it and make up your own mind.

Anyway, that finished my piano playing so I thought I would pull out Pom Pom's old clarinet. It was in pretty bad shape by then, so Dad offered to buy me a new one. We selected an excellent quality clarinet, but the retailer suggested to Dad that we would be wasting his time as my fingers did not fit over the keys of the instrument. He suggested we forget all about it. My father said, "that's not want me want to hear. What we want to know is how much would you charge to modify the keys to fit Ron's fingers." The music shop owner thought for a while and then quoted us fifteen pounds (about $30), which was no trouble at all. Dad accepted this offer and advised that I would be back on Friday to pick it up.

Thus followed many enjoyable musical experiences, joining in with the occasional visiting jazz band. By the

Jazz for 50th Birthday 8 Jan. 1986. Alan (U.K.) (trumpet), Dave Shore (drums), Ron (Clarinet), Greg Dawson (bass), Bob Anderson (piano).

early 1980's I was playing a regular Wednesday night gig in the Exchange Hotel in Kalgoorlie. These were some of the best nights of my life (perhaps my career has gone downhill ever since?). Our small group were fantastic, consisting of a strong trumpet player from England leading a very talented group (capable of supporting the clarinet player). Every Wednesday night I managed to squeeze out a few decent notes, just enough to get the creative juices flowing.

That period of my life ended when Greg Dawson, our keyboard player, was walking home one night, after playing with the band and he saw a bunch of drunken Aboriginals who were fighting each other and were out to kill each other. So, Greg stepped in and tried to separate them, but they knocked him over and kicked his head in. He died that night and that was really the end of our band.

You may have heard of Acker Bilk, a clarinet player of great renown. I first met him at the One Hundred Club (100 Oxford Street, London) when we were alongside each other at the urinal. We were standing there, as you do, and I thought, "I cannot believe it, Acker Bilk is standing next to me." I introduced myself and he replied with, "I'm Acker." I always remember we laughingly had to change hands to shake hands with each other (as was the pre-Covid custom).

Some years later Acker Bilk came to Kalgoorlie with his band and performed at the Kalgoorlie Town Hall. After his concert he was signing CD's and I spoke with him. I asked if he remembered meeting me under the earlier circumstances. He smiled and was kind enough to say he did.

I mention this because it relates to our Exchange Hotel jazz band. Our trumpet player, Alan, was particularly good, but he used to tell tall stories, making out he played with all the big bands in London and knew all the musicians. We suspected he was probably living in Kalgoorlie on the run from the Family Law Court in the UK or similar!

On the night of Acker Bilk's Kalgoorlie concert when Acker had finished signing CDs, Colin Smith (his trumpet player) said to me, "Acker is tired and wants to go to bed, but it's too early for me. Is there any jazz around here?" I replied, "Come with me and I will take you up to the

Exchange Hotel". It was a Wednesday night and Alan was playing our usual gig because he was the band leader (whereas I could take off for the night and go and listen to Acker Bilk). I was eagerly anticipating whether there would be any recognition because Colin Smith should have known all the London jazz musicians.

We burst in on the group at the Exchange Hotel, the room full of patrons and strippers – the whole works. Colin looks across the room and cries out, "Oh, it's fookin' Alan!" That night the hotel patrons witnessed some fine duelling trumpeters at work!

So, let me answer my earlier question of how I ended up playing the clarinet in Laverton in 1962. Benny Goodman was another famous clarinet player and Benny inspired me. In 1962 he went to Russia on a cultural exchange program to take jazz to the Russians. I said to myself, "If Benny Goodman can do that, then I can take my clarinet to Laverton and bring them some culture." My co-driver thought I was going to play one or two numbers and get back in the car. However, the assembled gathering there entered the true spirit of the occasion and Laverton was subjected to a full morning of enthusiastic antiphony which developed into a good sequence of call and answer type jazz. I recall the most popular number was Basin Street Blues.

So, what did I learn from that experience of my father not agreeing to have my arm taken off and of him saying to the music shop owner, "I don't want to hear about what doesn't fit, I want to hear about what you can do to make it fit?" They are two memories that stick with me, and I'm reminded of them each time I complete a task that is easier with two hands. Every time I do up my shoelaces up, I say, "Thanks Dad".

The moral of this story? Never take no for an answer. Listen to all the advice from the "experts" but always think carefully about who should make the final decision.

As Thomas Sowell once said, "It is hard to imagine a more stupid or more dangerous way of making decisions than by putting those decisions in the hands of people who pay no price for being wrong."

WHY WERE UKRAINE'S PRESIDENT ZELENSKYY'S SENIOR POLITICIANS AND ECONOMIC ADVISORS ZOOMING INTO OUR OFFICE IN PERTH, ON 28TH JUNE 2022?

Another accidental sequence of events. A long story, but I will try to be brief.

The sequence started in 2010, at the remarkable Atlas Network Liberty Forum in Washington DC.

The Atlas Network was started by Sir Antony Fisher AFC in 1981, and partners with over five hundred think tanks, all around the world.

Sir Antony died in 1988, but the Atlas Network continues to grow.

Now, what is the Atlas Network's connection with Ukraine?

Seven of the Atlas Network affiliate think tanks are based in Ukraine. (About the same number in Australia/New Zealand.)

In 2010 I was at an Atlas graduation ceremony for youth training in leadership, in Washington DC. Young people from all over the world participate and at the end of two weeks of training they give a sixty second 'Elevator Pitch' in front of all the attendees. We then voted for the best of these Elevator Pitches.

One young girl from Ukraine gave her pitch. I was right at the back of the room, and I thought wow; here is another Margaret Thatcher in the making. She just got up there and belted it to them as to what she was going to do with her life. I never saw her again at that conference, lost amongst the 320 attendees.

Perhaps she was gone forever?

However, by a strange coincidence, 2 years later at a Mont Pelerin Society meeting in Istanbul, I was running late to catch a tour coach as they were blowing their horn. There was only one seat left on the coach. So, I jumped in the seat, breathless from running late. To my astonishment, who was I seated with? It was this same girl from Ukraine, Yuliya. By the time we arrived back at our hotel, I do not know who said it first, but we decided to be friends forever.

So, that is what happens in this wonderful world of ideas.

Yuliya then, sometime later, started Skyping me. She had gone back to Ukraine, and with her youth network, were plotting how to remove Ukraine's current corrupt President (Yanukovych). She had established a group of approximately

Yuliya and Ron – Istanbul, Turkey Oct 2, 2011.

forty students, who then started marching in the street. I understand that Yuliya was up on the back of a truck with a megaphone doing her Margaret Thatcher stuff again. One night she contacted me, via Skype, and advised they had started with forty students marching, then the next night four hundred, then the President of Microsoft in Ukraine put a social media post up and they got ten thousand the next night.

Then a few nights later she advised that the Yanukovych government had just shot five of those students. The next night there were fifteen of the students shot. Pretty tough and unsettling stuff. Yuliya was bearing the heavy burden of leadership. To continue or backdown? Then the news that the government had closed down the blood bank so they could not even provide blood to the bleeding students. So, Yuliya, with her network, organized a team of taxis to travel to the regions and bring in the right quantities (and types) of blood to keep the youth 'revolution' going.

In the end, the government shot and killed over hundred students. There is now an avenue in Kyiv called The Alley of the Heavenly Hundred Heroes!

Alley of the Heavenly Hundred Heroes.

These brave young 'revolutionaries' maintained their courageous focus. They knew that if they backed down they would be forever stuck with crooked leadership. They kept up the Maidan Youth Revolution until Yanukovych, fled the country, never to return.

At that time (2014) I remember reflecting on the effectiveness of the Atlas Network's Leadership Academy Training and its ability to produce such measurable results.

Yuliya really earned her 'stripes' with that experience. Little did she realize that this brief period of rebuilding a 'better Ukraine' would be cut short by a full-scale war (in February 2022).

Now (2002), she is right in the middle of Ukraine's ongoing defence against Russia's aggression. Currently, Yuliya, and her three children, are living with my daughter in the English countryside. From there she is being flown in and out of Romania, United Arab Emirates and last weekend, Colorado, co-ordinating her war efforts from there.

Since the Russians cowardly attack on Feb. 24, 2022, Yuliya has flown to fifteen different countries as part of the Ukraine war effort (@ Nov 20, 2022) [Further update @ Nov 2023, a total of 75 return international flights.]

My two visits to Ukraine have left me with happy memories of friendly people, so I am angered by the current events. My first visit was to Yuliya and Roman's wedding, where she requested that I write and read some poems. These poems were of happier times, so let me share them with you. My Executive Assistant, Judy, when typing the poems said, "The first three poems are okay, but the fourth one is not suitable for a young girl's wedding." So, I rolled that one up and gave it to Yuliya the following day.

Poem #1 is *Toast to the New Generation (Yuliya & Roman)* pages 66/67 *Poems of Passion*:

TOAST TO THE NEW GENERATION
(Yuliya and Roman)

Each of you have been
busy these past years,
preparing for life,
casting aside any fears.

Yuliya, I saw in 2010,
giving a speech that showed
the many seeds she had gathered,
seeking fertile fields to be sowed.

Each time since, she has grown,
resembling a young Margaret Thatcher,
to serve her beloved Ukraine,
before some man could catch her.

Studying, reading, preparing,
absorbing wisdom both old and some new,
she was fully prepared
and knew just what to do.

Now to Roman we turn
an ideal balance to this team,
acquiring education and skills,
blending together it would seem.

An interesting education,
ranging from economics in Barcelona,
charity work, restaurants, and health care,
all essential parts of Roman's persona.

Roman always gets it right
but by his actions today,
breaks many Ukrainian hearts
in an unintentional way.

So for all of us here tonight,
we rely on your generation
to create a better world
and particularly for the Ukraine nation.

Roman is loved by Yuliya
and all her family,
in particular, by Sophiyka,
Yuliya's 8-year-old sister.

Sophiyka has proudly announced
that she aims to
grow up fast
so, she can marry Roman.

This introduced an element of urgency.
So that's why Yuliya
decided to speed things up
and today beats off all competition.

Now Sophiyka please bring me a drink,
so before we dance
let us all drink a toast
to Yuliya and Roman's fine romance.

Visualize that poem being read by me and translated by a Master of Ceremonies (MC) and also put up on a big screen. Halfway through the second poem Yuliya was not satisfied with the MC's interpretation of what I was saying so she came down, in her bridal outfit, snatched the microphone from the MC and delivered the poem with her own forceful interpretation.

This next is *The Year of the Horse – Page 68 Poems of Passion:*

THE YEAR OF THE HORSE
(Is it a good year for marriage?)

I asked my Chinese fortune teller,
In this Year of the Horse,
"is this a good year for marriage?"
He instantly replied, "of course!"

His reply was encouraging,
A very lucky year indeed.
Two healthy young horses,
moving forward at great speed.

They don't compete with each other,
growing at their own pace.
That way, both can win,
working together, instead of a race.

So you, two young horses,
galloping into the future,
doing everything quickly,
with energy, speed and stamina.

So, as you embark on your journey,
our best wishes are with you of course,
and we know you will travel safely,
in this lucky Year of the Horse

This third one is *If Only*, and I am glad she interpreted this one – *Page 69 Poems of Passion*:

IF ONLY

If only I were 50 years younger,
I'd smuggle you back to Australia.
But the future is yours,
as it rapidly unfolds.

You and I have work to do,
in our parts of the world.
So, we keep in touch,
as our adventures continue.

Now, this is the one my Executive Assistant thought was unsuitable *Fleeting Thoughts (Page 70, Poems of Passion:*

FLEETING THOUGHTS

When she reached around your neck,
to find the elusive clip
on your favourite bowtie –
seconds before the final click –
where were your thoughts?

She positioned parts of herself
upon your willing chest.
She was intent on fixing things –
but what were your thoughts?
Ah, give it a rest!

It was a moment's aberration
on your part, because you know
this friend, this friendship also has
the spark of light and joy in life
that is forever set to grow.

It is a friendship made to last.
Crafted with care by me and you.
It has brought me joy all of the past.
Now that your future is changing,
I hope that this friend stays part of it too.

> Bless you, dear friend
> and the bridegroom you've chosen.
> May your lives stay as joyous
> as the day of your Vesillya*.
> The best of good luck to you from Australia!

*Vesillya means wedding in Ukraine. 2014/05

My second visit to Ukraine was in 2016 as a speaker at the Free-Market Road Show (see Part 3 of this book).

Transporting myself from these happy times in 2014, to the war-torn times of November 2022, brings us to the intensity of what Ukraine is enduring as Russia relentlessly pursues its sub-human actions. On both my visits I was impressed with the young people of Ukraine, and I wonder how our young Australians would respond to a challenge like that? I do also wonder how we (the rest of the world) will be judged, by future generations, as we decide on our levels of support for Ukraine.

Coincidentally, in March 2022, the Institute of Public Affairs surveyed 1,000 Australians asking them: "If Australia was in the same position as Ukraine is now, would you stay and fight, or leave the country?" Of the Australians aged 18 to 24 surveyed, the results were:

- Stay and fight 32 per cent.
- Leave the country 40 per cent.
- Unsure 28 per cent.

What should we all be doing? Who amongst us has the wisdom to produce an instant solution? What I do know, is that I have been fortunate in earlier briefings, in that part of the world, to feel a sense of personal involvement. In 1990 I was selected to be part of the forty-person team sent to Russia. We were there to participate in the CATO Institute's "Transition to Russia's Freedom" training sessions. The purpose was to train the Russians on how to manage free enterprise because it was due to arrive shortly. As we prepared for our visit, we did not realize it would 'arrive' during the same weeks of our visit. They were pulling down statues, changing the names of cities and the entire process was pandemonium.

For the full story see Chapter 10. "The Seven Days that Shook the World" –

https://www.mannwest.com/the-lonely-libertarian/

So, it was the coincidence of my 1990 experience in Russia and, more recent contact with my Atlas contact, Yuliya, that led to the Zoom relationship with Ukraine's forward planning and Zoom Conference to Mannkal Foundation's, Perth (Subiaco) office. This partially answers the question I asked in this chapter's title.

(Further notes on my continuing friendship with Yuliya at the end of this chapter).

I first became interested in 'Government Policy' (and the outcomes of good versus bad policies) in 1973 during my time as President of the Chamber of Commerce in Kalgoorlie. We tired of seeing the materials and equipment, ordered for the operating of the mining industry, coming through Kalgoorlie, non-stop, on the train. However, we were not permitted to take them off the train. It had to go on to Perth (another day's travel) and then be brought back, some three and a half weeks later to Kalgoorlie.

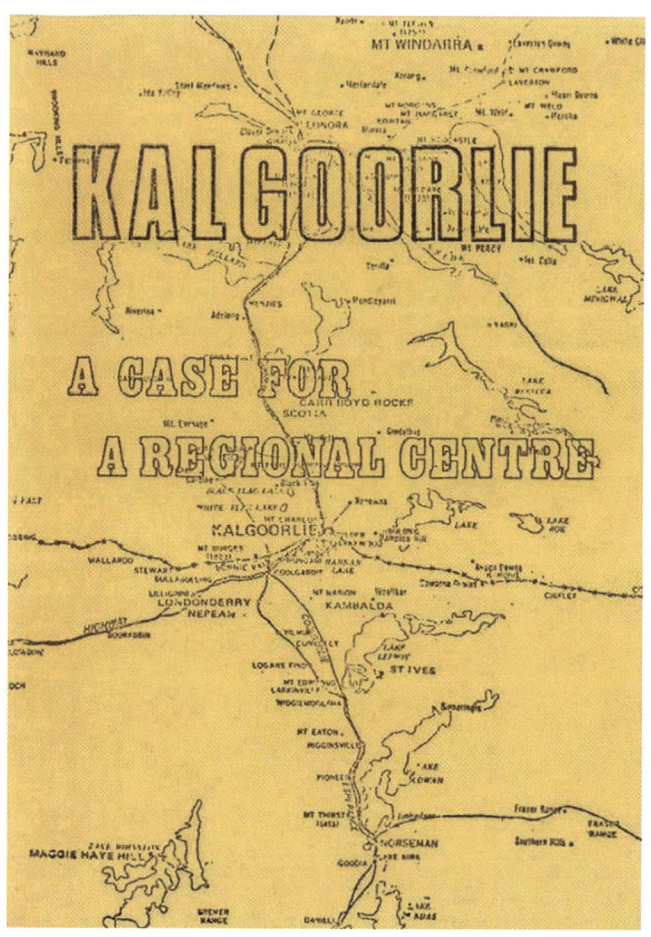

https://www.mannwest.com/wp-content/uploads/2023/10/Kalgoorlie-A-case-for-a-Regional-Centre.pdf

We could not see the logic in this 'Government Policy' ('protecting' their government monopoly railway) so, we developed a case for Kalgoorlie to become a 'Regional Centre'.

So, we were successful in breaking the railway monopoly strangle-hold. Now the materials go directly to Kalgoorlie, for off-loading onto road transport straight up to the Pilbara or other numerous mine sites. If you can save a month it has a huge result on costs to run a mine. Some of the 'down time' mining equipment costs can be $1M per hour. So, to survive, you have to keep a mine operating.

More recently (2012), our Mannkal Foundation, developed a document entitled Project Western Australia which is a listing of policies including health, transport, education, etc. and any time there is a State election, we update and circulate this to every State politician in the hope that they might read it and learn something. Unfortunately, there is not a lot of take-up from our politicians. They are 'followers' rather than 'leaders' and they see few votes to be gained by pursuing productive reforms.

Refer to our latest (2021) edition (cover image right) of *Project Western Australia* – https://www.mannkal.org/research-publications/project-wa/

During 2022, the Atlas Network heard about our publication, obtained copies, and sent them to Ukraine with the idea that they might consider translating it to use as a model for planning the economic rebuild of Ukraine.

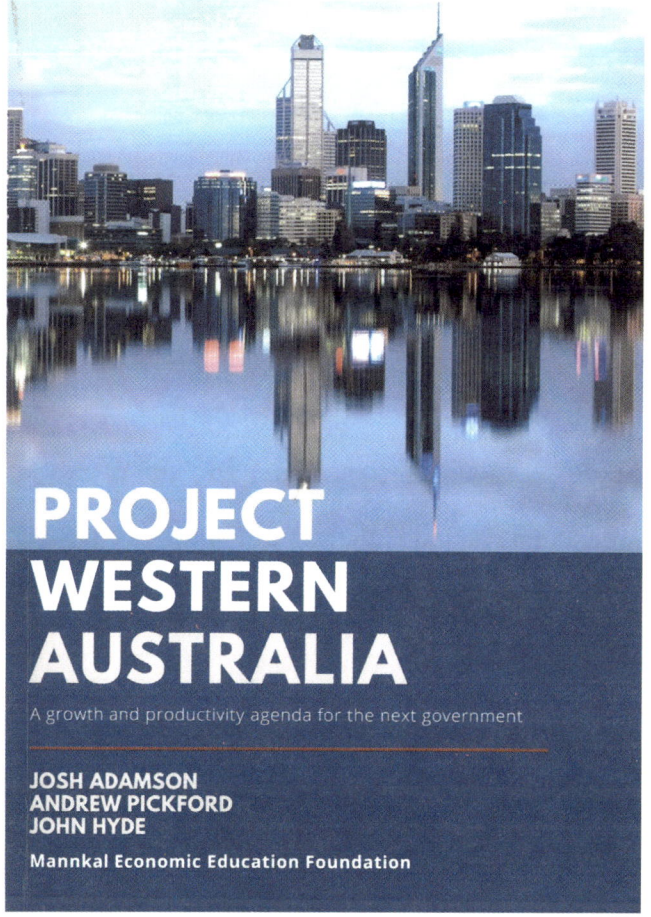

It is imperative that they start planning now, for the end of the war, and this time (unlike 1991) learning to get their 'privatization' right.

Russia also bungled their 'privatisation' and I remember James Buchanan, the Nobel Prize Winning Economist, who was with our 1990 group in Russia, saying, "This is not going to work out well, as explained by Public Choice Theory. The real assets of Russia are going to fall into the hands of the few (oligarchs later became the word) that receive concentrated benefits, and they will work their hardest, to make sure this happens, and the poor 'suckers' out there who think they are going to benefit from a free market will get nothing." He was absolutely correct.

In former Soviet Union countries, and I have been to many including Lithuania, Estonia, etc. When they privatized it all happened in a hurry. If you owned an apartment on the fourth floor of a Soviet-built block of apartments that apartment became yours. That cubic space was yours. That was your 'Property Right'.

Now, 30 to 40 years later, those buildings were never built well and are now deteriorating. You cannot demolish them to rebuild, because the 'owners' would lose everything. They will lose their 'space'. When they privatized, they did not allow the people to own part of the underlying land asset. That was still owned by the government. Something we do have in Western Australia is the Strata Title Act to protect against and manage multi-owner properties. However, we did not have that until about 1968. It is a useful form of legislation that enables peaceful management of communal properties. None of that existed in Russia or Ukraine. A copy of our Strata Title Act is currently being studied in Ukraine.

The leaders in Ukraine are determined to get their privatisation right this time, despite there being a war on. They are preparing for the end of the war. Helping us, help

Ukraine, with good policies is Robert Stevens (the former Registrar of the Western Australian Mines Department). He knows that our West Australian Mining Act is the best in the world. Ukraine now has a copy of this Mining Act, and they are currently studying it, modifying, and translating it. As a result, they too will have one of the best Mining Acts in the world.

So, there you have the full story of how President Zelenskyy's advisors were zooming in to our office on 28 June 2022.

Ukraine's Ambassador to Australia, His Excellency Mr Vasyl Myroshnychenko discovered a tree planted in 1895. The same age as the Manners/Mannwest family firm.

Now, let me finish with another poem. Dedicated to Australia's productive few with a connection to the mining industry because many of you could have, at some stage, a connection with Australia's great resource industry. This 2016 item from my book *Poems of Passion (pages 84 – 85, 2016).*

CHARACTER BEATS STRATEGY (EVERY TIME)

Here we go again.
A strategy for this,
a strategy for that.

Most of our 'thought leaders',
spend their time,
talking through their hat.

What we really need,
is to focus on courage,
conviction and character.

This gave our Western Civilisation
that special edge.
Lifting millions to a new level.

The Enlightenment thinking,
Isaac Newton and friends,
blazed the trails.

Before Entitlements and Victimhood,
ran us
off the rails.

In Canberra, this week,
I was told Canberra
is our National Capital.
"Wrong!", I said.
"It's merely
our Political Capital."

I define Canberra
as 200 square kilometers;
surrounded by reality!

Canberra is where
they work hard to
destroy our Triple A Credit Rating.

It's 'out there'.
You are the people
working to save it?

You the creators,
will rescue us,
from political seduction.

So, let's drink a festive toast.

To the explorers,

Our industry and our great producers.

Footnote on friendship:

Many years ago, a youthful acquaintance of mine used these words to describe me, I never knew whether she was insulting me or complimenting me:-

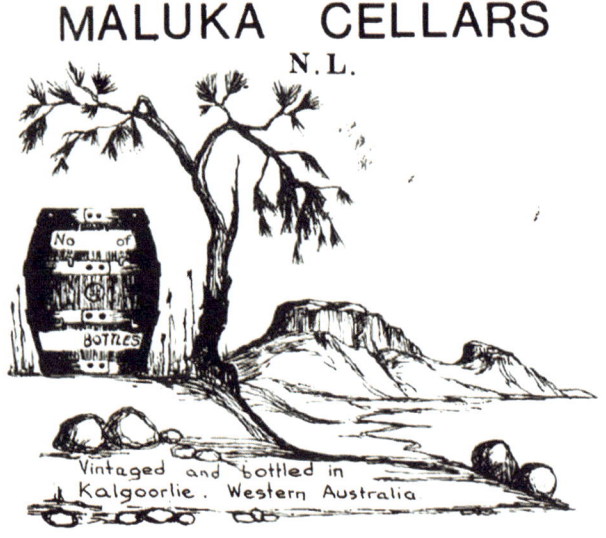

"He was a man who understood the oddity, the eccentricity of life and he would always respond to whatever it was in a situation that promised to make it greater than its circumstances."—D.S.

Each time I meet up with Yuliya (at the occasional economic conference around the world) I am reminded of these words as our simple meetings seemed to develop into something grander than anticipated.

An example being a quick Italian meal together in Guatemala (November 2021). The Guatemala 'Italian Restaurant' proprietor lady, being confused with our two entirely different English accents enquired what we were doing in Guatemala. Upon hearing that we were attending a Mont Pelerin Society Meeting at the Francisco Marroquin University (UFM), she proclaimed loudly that her husband was a graduate and proceeded to fetch him... and her husband joined us... and

more family members joined us!

Then, under further interrogation, they were amazed to discover that we knew the founder of the university. They then explained how the UFM had played a major part in educating their expanded family.

On this discovery they then 'put out the word' and we were quickly surrounded by an ever-expanding family group.

Our quick Italian meal for two rapidly developed into a comprehensive family reunion, for the rest of the evening.

That is why I always look forward to my next brief meeting with Yuliya, as I never quite know how these impromptu events will end up. In anticipation, or perhaps a combination of anticipation and apprehension?

Note: This chapter was based on my speech at The Royal Sydney Golf Club on 11 Jul 2022. Hosted by Mr James Walker – former Mannkal scholar and now Member of The Mont Pelerin Society.

PART 3

THE FREE MARKET ROAD SHOW (EUROPE'S EIGHTH WONDER OF THE WORLD?)

An enjoyable annual experience is participating in this masterpiece of logistical organisation. Being one of their panel, of over one hundred speakers, who as if by magic find themselves 'curated' into groups of approximately four. Their overall participation in thirty-eight cities, over forty four days, leaves me in awe that everything proceeds with immaculate precision.

Each speaker might average four destinations, each with different members.

From the Free Market Road Show's own documents:-

ABOUT THE FREE MARKET ROAD SHOW™ (FMRS)

Network and Vision.

Spearheaded by the Austrian Economics Center FMRS is built on trust and respect, on the voluntary, deliberate collaboration of more than 100 universities, groups and selected individuals to widely spread individual and entrepreneurial freedom, focusing on solutions to today's problems.

FMRS creates awareness for the importance to constantly defend freedom. Experts from different fields and regions provide comprehensive explanations for the nuances of economic freedom in flexible formats with low-threshold access. The onfy drug against the toxic influence of populistic and centrolistic ideas and irresponsible policies is public awareness.

Academy of Freedom.

The FMRS Family's continuous ambition to build new networks and coalitions helps spread the message of individual and entrepreneurial freedom, sound policy, self responsibility and – not least – free speech to new audiences. By showcasing a diverse range of perspectives, FMRS ensures that the discourse remains balanced and informed. This is particulary pertinent for the younger generation, who are often exposed to a singular narrative. Through the FMRS, they gain access to a broader spectrum of ideas, fostering critical thinking and a deeper appreciation for economic principles. By weaving the principles of freedom into every disicussion and solution. FMRS serves as an academy of freedom, educating and inspiring it's participants.

History.

FMRS was launched in 2008, as a platform for economic discourse and by 2017, the FMRS was touring an impressive 45 cities across Europe and additional 5 stops in the US.

2020 and 2021 reaching a global online audience and keeping the network align and operating.

2022 FMRS was back on the road, reviving in-person engagements.

2023 subsequent stops in Israel set the stage for the European and US tours.

For more information, please see: – *bttps://freemarket-rs.com/ and the latest report https://freemarket-rs.com/wp-content/uploads/2023/10/FMRS-Long-2023.pdf*

The following pages cover my three-city sampler from my participation in the 2023 tour;

- Estonia (Entrepreneurship).
- Bratislava (Reliable Energy Sources for Citizens & Industry).
- Warsaw / Kyiv (Designing Policies for the Post-War Reconstruction).

TALLINN – ESTONIA – THE HOME OF ENTREPRENEURSHIP

Starting at the Bottom (I am still not sure where I will end up) *Free Market Road Show – Tallinn by* **Ron Manners***, 26 April 23.* I am told that when talking to a group of entrepreneurs they will not listen if they think you are an academic.

Entrepreneurs only learn from entrepreneurs.

Entrepreneurship is a 'mindset' rather than a 'science'.

Let me tell you, that I was an entrepreneur even before I knew how to spell the word entrepreneur.

At age 12, I was making and selling Crystal Sets (the precurser of the transistor radio). Then, at age 15, after school, I ran a very profitable business where you might say that "I started at the bottom".

I need to give you a picture here of a circa-1950s Australian toilet a 'dunny'.

Back in the day, there was no plush, double-ply toilet paper as we know it today.

This was before the invention of the toilet paper in rolls.

It was then a custom to use old magazines or newspapers, then along came the toilet roll, with which you are all familiar.

Well, there was one problem, I always seemed to be getting the very last piece of paper so, I did something about it. I invented the dual roll holder – perhaps the first of its kind in the world? (I may never know).

Well, what do you know, it took Australia by storm, each day after school I tended to my 'production line'. I had a small device that easily bent the steel frame and welded it to a hook-hole.

On the left of the picture, you see the frames hanging, after spray painting and, on the right, you see the weekly advertisement which ran in a national magazine.

Business was brisk, everyone seemed to want one as a worthy addition to their bathroom.

This dual roll holder and magazine rack was marketed as the 'Seatside Companion'.

This was a very elegant contraption. They became both a fashion statement and a national icon.

Some people would take the Seatside Companion for a walk, more stylish than a dog!

Others just hung them in their library.

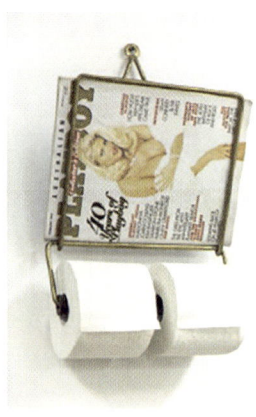 

You might ask, why am I not still in this profitable business? Well, I read somewhere, that if you run a business for too long, you end up looking just like it. So, it was time to move on from this business at the 'bottom'. But, just before moving on let me give you some statistics. The price of the Seatside Companion was A$3.00, including postage anywhere in Australia. Just for comparison I took my remaining device to Australia Post, recently, and found that it would now cost $20, just to mail it anywhere in Australia.

I calculated that there has been a ten times increase in the price over these 70 years. The price really has not gone up; it is just that the government has destroyed our money by a factor of ten. Our government is just like most governments, having got themselves into debt, they find the best way out is to declare 'partial bankruptcy' by destroying the currency, in effect, paying their creditors ten cents in the dollar.

Yes, I have little confidence in governments when they stray from their very few legitimate roles.

Well, I may have started at the 'bottom' but, I have managed to repeat that entrepreneurial pattern, many times, over my long life.

- I brought the first jukebox to my city.
- I imported from Turkey a spectacular salt-eating plant, 'Puccinellia' that rehabilitated Australia's salt-damaged pasture lands.
- Our family mining equipment company has been actively involved in Australian mining for 128 years and, over that time, we have done many entrepreneurial exercises. One being to convert many of Australia's mine winders from steam-driven to electric.

Plate 6.2.167 Mt. Charlotte - Reward Shaft. Drivers controls

In the 1970s underground mining was done with a man-operated 'bogger' like the one illustrated below. Then the price of nickel collapsed, and many mines were running at a loss.

Plate 5.4.18 Rocker Shovel - Chaffers.
This is a Joy type working on the 3000ft (914m) level.

I wondered how Sweden was managing to mine extremely low grades of underground iron ore and transport by rail, over the mountains, through the export port of Narvik in Norway. To follow up my curiosity, I flew to Sweden and went underground at every Swedish mine, from Lapland in the North, right through to the south of Sweden.

I found that by 'scaling up' they had overcome their lack of grade by use of large Kiruna diesel dump trucks. They managed to get an incredibly low profile, for operating in the underground mines, by putting two Volvo engines, side-by-side, and the diesel exhaust, which would normally be unsafe for use underground was run through catalytic converters (cylinders containing millions of platinum prils). They had used science to overcome this significant technical problem.

We imported many millions of dollars-worth of these trucks and the nickel mines maintained profitability.

That gives me confidence that right now, in 2023, we could continue to use science to overcome engine exhaust emissions that are being presented to us as being of 'Crisis proportions'. There is plenty of scope for entrepreneurs in this field and a much better plan for the world's economy than the green extremists' demands that we shut down our industries.

Let me conclude this series of entrepreneurial mini adventures by mentioning our successful importation, from England, of the 'disposable steel rock bits', back in around 1950.

We were selling these 'disposable rock bits' (they just fitted on the end of a tapered drill steel and once they became blunt you just knocked them off and fitted another).

We were selling these by the thousands until one day this all stopped.

The Swedes invented a tungsten insert which they fitted into the steel rod which became an integrated steel rod with a tungsten insert. This certainly outlasted our 'disposable product' and our market disappeared instantly. What was I to do with 20,000 of the old disposable rock bits?

Would I spend the rest of my life looking at shelves full of these unwanted rock bits? At about that time I had been curious at a particular metal usage, and I noted that Australia's fishing industry was a major user of lead. What for, I asked? Upon checking I found that they were pouring lead into small moulds in which was embedded a wire loop.

Plate 5.2.11 "P.M." Bits – North Kalgurli These were some experimental "throw-away" type 1950). There were several types of bit and variations to the rod.

These were then used all the way around Australia's fishing nets. After a little more investigation I found that each of these lead weights were about the same weight as our rock bits, which also featured a convenient hole.

Another market miraculously opened, and I was happily able to sell the unwanted 'bits' at a much higher price than the mining industry had been prepared to pay.

Not all of my entrepreneurial efforts have been this successful and I even wrote a book about all my spectacular failures, yes, the title of the book was *Heroic Misadventures*

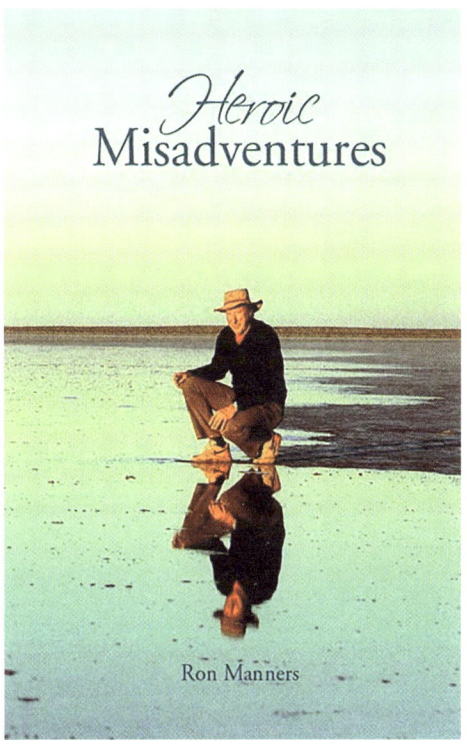

Free e-book available here –

https://www.mannwest.com/books/heroic-misadventures/

So spectacular were my failures, that my book was a sell-out success. Could you imagine that; I made good money from selling a book about my failures?

Anyway... that brings us right up to 2023 where I am more excited about the future of entrepreneurship than I have ever been, over those many years.

THE GOOD NEWS

One of the greatest drivers for the entrepreneurial start-up industry is the current fad or cult of E.S.G. (Environment,

Sustainability, Governance) and D.E.I. (Diversity, Equity, Inclusion).

Anyone who has studied economics and, in particular, Public Choice Theory will immediately recognize this fad as being a money-making scheme by those receiving the 'Concentrated Benefits', with the costs 'widely dispersed' over an unsuspecting public.

This cult or fad will continue on its merry way until some current class actions from aggrieved shareholders, give a jolt to public company boards who have been seduced by the warm fuzzy language of E.S.G. and D.E.I.

The strange thing is that most good companies already practise this good governance, necessary for corporate longevity, and have no need to demote 'profitability' from the major priority of their enterprise.

The good news is that shareholders are 'fleeing' to private equity and unlisted companies and find the new start-up industry attractive, in this respect. Let us enjoy this redirection of shareholders funds while it lasts.

So, what am I doing about it?

After a lifetime of taking risks, with a better rate of success than failure, I can recognize the mind-set that mark the successful entrepreneurs.

I am not an investment advisor and I'm not putting forward these three most interesting start-up/venture companies, in any way other than suggesting you should look closely at their style of operation.

The three of them are geographically well separated:-
- Bombora – Investment Management Partners (Sydney – Australia) *https://www.bomboragroup.com.au/*
- Purpose Ventures (Perth – Australia) *https://www.purpose.ventures/*
- Startup Wise Guys (Tallinn – Estonia) *https://startupwiseguys.com/*

You will find no preoccupation with E.S.G./D.E.I. language amongst this group but, you will get an insight into the skilled entrepreneurship that the world urgently requires to lift it out of the E.S.G./D.E.I. swamp and its self-serving jargon.

BRATISLAVA – TALKING OF ENERGY

Free Market Road Show – Bratislava – Slovakia by **Ron Manners**, *26 April 2023.*

Here we are in Bratislava (Slovakia) talking about energy and providing citizens with reasonably priced, and most importantly, reliable energy.

We could be anywhere in the world with a similar discussion but, the most adversely effected countries are those who have followed the mass hysteria of climate catastrophism. US$1.4 trillion has been spent, so far, on promoting so-called renewable green energy, with two results:-

1. Energy has become threateningly expensive.
2. A switch to renewables has increased by 1% (14% to 15%).

While we, the free world, have been closing down coal and nuclear power stations[5], China has been building more coal-fired economical power stations than the rest of the world, all put together.

The world has become alarmingly dependant on China, for manufactured goods, to the same extent that Europe became alarmingly dependant on Russia for reliable energy.

Just before I left Australia I had a look around our office and our home to see if there was anything not made in China. Yes, I found one thing! Our toothpaste was made in Poland!

Just a word on Australia, as few of you may have visited.

Australia (The land of Net Zero = Net Wisdom)

Despite being the greatest country in which to live, most of us are so busy enjoying ourselves that we do not spend enough time reflecting on the many good reasons why people from all over this world, choose Australia when they decide to flee from all-too-common dysfunctional authoritarian

[5] https://www.skynews.com.au/opinion/paul-murray/power-stations-blown-up-as-renewables-take-over/video/0ff4e72128b12fd2971e2f116cbe5fea

political systems.

Yes, we are influenced by the Marxist Antonio Gramsci's *Long March Through the Institutions*[6], but there are remnants enough of limited government and the Rule of Law, to enable us to successfully overcome the many obstacles to progress. Australia has much to learn about the art of providing citizens with reasonably priced and reliable energy and I am here to collect ideas to take back to Australia.

Australia has the natural energy resources (natural gas, coal, and uranium) to fill the huge supply gap created by current world events. But, instead of stepping forward and taking our place as responsible energy providers to the world, we are navel gazing as we are barely able to supply our domestic needs and existing export contracts, of natural gas, in particular.

We are caught up in a 'debate with ourselves', where there are few winners. How could this be, you ask? I will try not to turn this into a comedy, as my story is difficult to believe.

For today, in addition to my personal non-technical comments, I will also append some serious links for you to follow, in your own time.

Hopefully, this information will contribute some substance to your own considerations and planning, toward overcoming this energy challenge.

No country is alone in having to face this challenge.

[6] https://www.mannwest.com/has-the-crisis-industry-become-australias-greatest-threat/

The choice is between sane, rational decision making and 'populism', as that is how many of the issues must be resolved. Let me start with a chart, showing Australia's historic electricity prices 1955 – 2018.

We appeared to be doing very well until two events occurred.

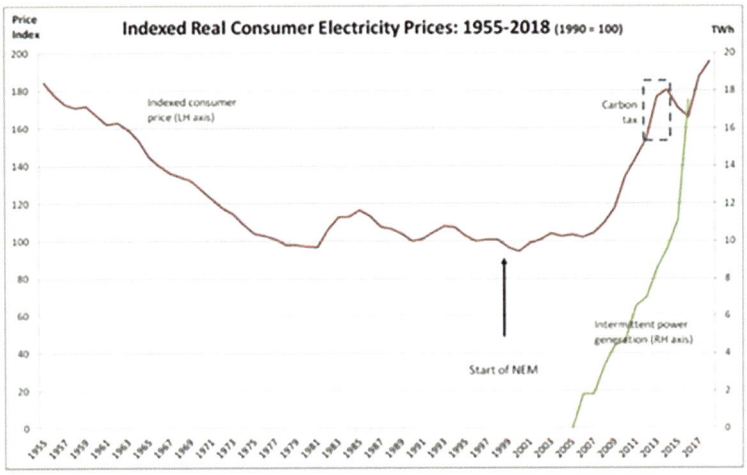

1. The establishment of the government's National Electricity Market.
2. The compulsory imposition of renewables.

That chart shows the challenge facing us in Australia to 'tame the escalating prices' of energy.

When I say Australians are debating with themselves, they are more like at war with themselves. I should explain that Australia started as a penal colony for the British and that is where our tendency toward over-government started.

THE FREE MARKET ROAD SHOW

The British brought more jailers and administrators than prisoners. Now, over two hundred years later, half of the population is trying to 'have a go' (as we say) and the other half is trying to shut us down.

To succeed in business, or in any field in Australia, you need to study and practise the strategies developed by Niccolo Machiavelli.

Machiavelli explains so well, just how those who seek to control and manipulate us, need to continually devise

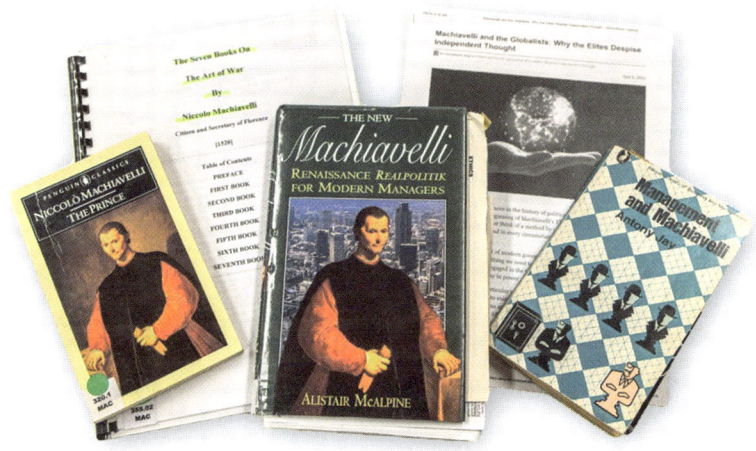

methods by which we become dependent on those very same people.

If you understand this process you can side-step such pressures and continue on your productive and merry way.

Let me give you two examples. Both stories involve Australia's leading energy company, Woodside Energy.

My first story goes right back to its beginnings in 1954.

My second story is from last week (April, 2023).

When Woodside started quite modestly with an issued capital of just $2M, their first Managing Director, Reece Withers, built a track through the coastal swamp and a footbridge over a small tidal inlet.

They needed that footbridge to establish a drilling platform and to commence drilling.

Then someone told Withers that he had not obtained a permit to build that footbridge, and when it was discovered, Woodside would be forced to remove it and lose access to the drill rig.

In true Machiavellian style, Withers called an inspector to the site, to ask permission to build a footbridge ten metres from the existing footbridge.

The inspector had a look around and triumphantly declared that he would never give permission for the footbridge to be built, because it was too close to the "existing bridge".

The inspector went away happy (flushed with power), and Woodside continued their drilling with remarkable success and is now a $64 Billion, super successful company. (How a $2M company becomes A$64B company.)

Machiavellian strategies were again required last week (April 2023) when the Woodside Chairman had to stand up to proxy activists (ESG motivated groups, including Labor Union controlled superannuation funds who were accusing Woodside of 'repeated failure to present a credible strategy to address climate change').

Nothing short of closing down the natural gas industry will satisfy those on the left. The extreme government pressure being imposed on Australia's natural gas industry are to be seen at[7].

The Australian Labor Party is dependent on the extreme Green Party, whose leader, Adam Bandt, says, "Labor seems 'more afraid' of the coal and gas corporations than 'climate collapse'."

Let us pause, for a moment, and examine these words. What is "climate collapse"?

The climate has been changing forever and will continue to do so but what exactly is "climate collapse'?

'Climate Collapse is the language of fear' used by the enemies of civilized society.

'Fear' is their weapon. In much the same way that Putin blows up hospitals and schools. That creates much more 'fear' than blowing up military targets, like tanks.

If we recognize 'fear', as today's weapon, we can develop strength to resist.

I could talk forever on the so-called climate debate, but for anyone undecided please listen to Al Gore to hear one side of the story and then have a listen to Australia's Prof. Ian Plimer or America's Mark P. Mills (Manhattan Institute).

If you have studied the economic subject of Public Choice Theory, you can recognize how those receiving the

[7] https://www.lexology.com/r.ashx?l=A03XUKS

'concentrated benefits', work so hard for their cause and how they carefully (Machiavellian style) off-load the costs to the unsuspecting millions of consumers, like us.

Yes, we are Conservationists. I'm sure that we are all conservationists at heart. I know, that with a background of farming and mining, I am. For every tree that I have cut down I have grown more than 100.

The reason I am a conservationist is simply that 'I live here too!'. In the mid-1970s I imported the first low-profile diesel trucks for operating in underground mines in Australia.

The platinum-filled exhaust scrubbers produced breathable exhaust air. I have continuing faith in the march of science to conquer challenges like this.

Yes, we will move to electric vehicles, in our own time, when it is appropriate. That time will be different for each of us, depending on our circumstances and where we live.

There can never be a legislated answer that suits us all.

As a colleague of mine, one of Australia's leading engineers, Peter Iancov – *https://www.zinfra.com.au/about/people/peter-iancov* – has recently visited Europe and produced a report *European Energy Insights*. With his permission, I share this report with you[8]. His summary is as follows:

"**Energy security** is key to civilisation in Europe is particularly prominent. Most countries have found a way to secure

[8] https://www.mannwest.com/wp-content/uploads/2023/04/European-Energy-Insights-LT-Report_pi_for_rm.pptx

alternative sources from the Russian gas and to some extent are continuing to diversify. Italy in particular secured alternative gas supplies from other sources including import terminals.

Energy transition: is not focussing on full electrification. To some extent we in Australia seem to be out of synch with the rest of the world. The European energy regulator is seeking 55% electrification away from fossil fuels. There might be a debate within EU if 45% or 65% is the right target but no one is targeting 100% as we seem to do in Australia. Nuclear and Gas generation are considered 'green' and counted as solutions.

Regulatory regime: it is better in Europe and the relationship with energy producers and transporters is a lot closer and more collaborative to ensure significant incentives are applied to key drivers like customers safety, service, reliability, availability, and cost.

Customer service: front of mind with a genuine focus to support the customer and earn the incentives attached to it. Improvements are rewarded and whilst there are penalties that apply, their application threshold is a lot lower than in Australia. That may change one day, but so far business is incentivised to perform not penalised.

Digitalisation: core activity that enables data analysis and usage to support improvements. Costs are rarely challenged by the Regulator, and they become part of the tariff calculation formulas in most cases.

Risk: all future capital work is delayed due to supply chain availability. Securing supply channels for plant and equipment is paramount including for mega companies like Enel with a customer pool three timesthe size of Australian population. Resourcing is of some concern but not a lot since the rules of moving people across utilities and countries seem to be a lot easier that transferring tradesmen from Queensland to Victoria."

The other two pressures being imposed on Australia's natural gas industry are:-
- Lexology: Last minute Safeguard Mechanism Reforms[9].
- Bans on fracking.
- Bans on onshore gas exploration.
- Potential restrictions on exports of LNG.
- Potential price caps on domestic gas.

Yes, we can work toward net-zero emissions, but we will never get there without the help of natural gas, hydro, hydrogen, batteries, and nuclear power.

All these options must be encouraged to vigorously compete for our business (without distortions of government subsidies) and, may the best economic answer be the winner!

[9]https://www.lexology.com/r.ashx?l=A03XUKS Clean Energy in Chicago (Why Windy Suburbs matter) - https://youtu.be/d5hu62W89nk

WARSAW – KYIV – ECONOMIC REFORMS (REBUILDING AN ECONOMY)

Economic reforms and making them stick.

Free Market Road Show – Warsaw, Poland (As it was not possible to hold this event in Ukraine) by **Ron Manners**, *27 April 2023.*

My good news for you today, is this. "It only takes one person to change your country, or perhaps your world."

Most of you are aware of the damage done by one individual, the Marxist strategist Antonio Gramsci –

https://www.mannwest.com/has-the-crisis-industry-become-australias-greatest-threat/

You may not be aware that it was one person who saw the benefits to flow from the free market policies brought to Hong Kong.

It was Sir John Cowperthwaite[10], the Financial Secretary of Hong Kong, who installed an economic system so engrained in Hong Kong's policy setting that even China is having trouble unstitching it.

A study of John Cowperthwaite's policies and the outcome is worth careful study.

You may also not be aware of an example of how one person master-minded the economic reforms in New Zealand in the early 1980s. Roger Kerr[11] was his name and he inspired

---

[10] https://www.cato.org/commentary/sir-john-cowperthwaite-personal-tribute?utm_source=social&utm_medium=email&utm_campaign=Cato%20Social%20Share

[11] https://www.coordinationproblem.org/2011/11/roger-kerr-1945-2011.html

two courageous and determined New Zealand Members of Parliament (Roger Douglas and Ruth Richardson) to turn his policies into reality.

This gave the world an excellent example of how a free economy, and free people, can lift a country, and its people, quickly up the ladder of prosperity.

Bert Kelly[12], an Australian farmer and later, Member of Parliament, watched this happen and wondered if Australia could replicate this success story. Bert Kelly was a lone voice for much of his life, poking fun at the shackles of protectionism which throttled progress in New Zealand and Australia, for most of last century.

John Hyde, another farmer, from Western Australia, caught this 'economic reform bug' from Bert Kelly and it was John Hyde OAM[13] who constructed the detailed reforms, over every aspect of Australia's economy, which would lift our country.

He had assistance from others in his group (referred to as the 'Dries') but single-handedly he master-minded Australia's reform program from beginning to end.

As a Member of Parliament, John Hyde was unable to convince his own Liberal Prime Minister, Malcolm Fraser, to adopt any of these policies. But, surprisingly, the newly elected Labor Party Prime Minister, Bob Hawke, was convinced by John Hyde that these reforms, instituted

---

[12] https://www.mannwest.com/books/the-modest-member-the-life-and-times-of-bert-kelly/
[13] https://www.spectator.com.au/2023/01/former-liberal-mp-john-hyde-awarded-oam/

immediately, would establish Bob Hawke's reputation in the longer term.

Prime Minister, Bob Hawke, accepted John Hyde's program with enthusiasm and announced to his Cabinet, "We will do the lot".

From a personal point of view, it was my good fortune to be in business, at that time, and experienced our country – Australia – being 'set free'. Australia was just like a becalmed boat starved for wind suddenly receiving an enthusiastic full wind in our sails.

AUSTRALIA'S EXPLORATION & MINING – 1960 to 2015

Blue	=	Stockbrokers use this graph to show ASX Index.
Red	=	Adjusted for inflation (reality).
Gold	=	Price.

The full implications of John Hyde's contribution to Australia's reforms were captured in one document –

https://www.mannwest.com/john-hyde-in-three-words/

John Hyde's archives are available here –

https://www.mannkal.org/research-publications/john-hyde-archives/

These have been collected and include thousands of his regular newspaper articles detailing the economic challenges and the results from sensible reforms.

John Hyde inspired our Mannkal Foundation to produce a book – *Project Western Australia (A Growth and Productivity Agenda for the Next Government)* that was circulated, in print form, to every Western Australian politician and the media. This is available here in electronic form –

https://www.mannkal.org/wp-content/uploads/2021/02/PROJECT-WA-2021-ONLINE.pdf

Copies of our *Project Western Australia* were forwarded to Ukraine, last year, under the guidance of Tom Palmer from the Atlas Network and formed the basis of our extensive communications and Zoom conference with Maryan Zablotskyy, a Member of the Ukraine Parliament. We were also able to submit several sample copies of Australian legislation where various updates had overcome some problems of earlier legislation.

Now, all that sounds fairly simple, and it reminds me that all things do not go well, such as the collapse of the former Soviet Union.

In September 1990 as a Member of the CATO Institute

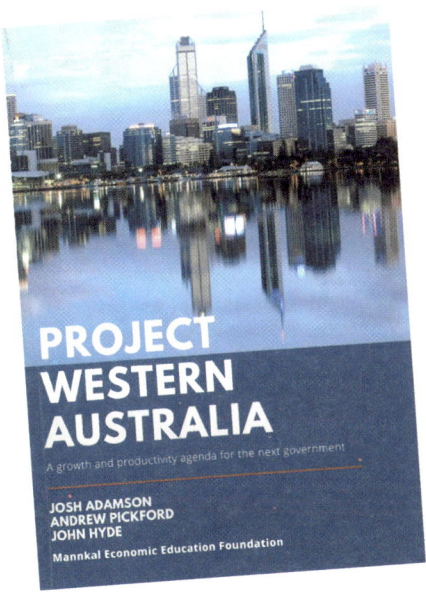

All successful Australian governments have implemented a set of wide-ranging microeconomic reforms which have enabled current and future generations to flourish. Western Australia's next government has a unique but limited opportunity to follow this example and to drive the next wave of prosperity. Now more than ever, Western Australia needs a government which leads microeconomic reform rather than reying on high iron ore prices and federal spending. Project WA takes a close look at the state's economy in order to provide a policy platform for a free, rich and globally prominent Western Australia.

visiting team to Russia and St. Petersburg, we held a large conference called *Transition to Freedom*.

At that time, we had the opportunity to physically see the Soviet Union falling to pieces. All this gave us, as free market proponents from the West, was a false sense of jubilation.

Let me quote from a Foundation for Economic Education publication, *Beware of Despair*, by their President, Hans F. Sennholz, in 1994, where he stated – "A free-market counterrevolution is rising, sweeping away socialism in all its forms and colours, and bringing hope to poor people everywhere. Governments are being downsized, public enterprises are privatized, and taxes are lowered. The 'houses' which Marx and Keynes built are being razed and replaced by 'houses' designed by Adam Smith and Ludwig von Mises. The light of economic freedom is shining brighter now than at any time in this century."

Yes, it was an easy trap for us to rejoice that the free market had won the battle of ideas!

This was to under-estimate the ongoing March of Gramsci's 'The Long March Through our Institutions'.

Similarly, the remarkable free-market steps made by New Zealand and Australia did not persist and anyone trying to start a new business, in either of those countries today, risk being overwhelmed by the weight of bureaucratic tentacles that inhibit any forward movement.

What have we learnt from this failed experiment to free the world's economy from the continuing overreach of governments and their attached bureaucracies?

If we are again successful in introducing free-market reforms what should be foremost in our minds?

How to make economic reforms stick!

For advice on locking in such reforms on a permanent basis it is of utmost importance to adopt the strategies outlined by Niccolo Machiavelli.

If you are not familiar with Machiavelli's strategies start here – https://quadrant.org.au/magazine/2023/03/australia-could-use-a-machiavelli-gary-furnell/ It is important to absorb and follow the content of the collection of Machiavellian links listed on page 142.

Now, with some background the importance of Machiavellian strategies, to lock in long-term reforms, it is time for me to hand over to my colleague and fellow director of the Mont Pelerin Society, Prof. Nils Karlson, of the Ratio Institute of Sweden.

In Prof. Karlson's book – *Statecraft and Liberal Reform in Advanced Democracies* – he covers, in detail, the economic reforms executed in various democracies and gives expert advice on making such reforms permanent.

For Prof. Karlson's full deck of illustration slides see Ref.[14]

So, in conclusion, I have stressed the importance of developing and instituting sweeping economic reforms to free up economies, in all our countries.

Of equal importance, is to focus on the strategies required to make those economic reforms permanent this time.

I have also outlined that these reforms are often brought into being by the work of one individual.

My challenge, therefore, to you is to either become that one person or to discover and support such a person in your country. Give them your fully focused support.

Equally important is to adopt strategies that will lock in and make it impossible for the reforms to be undone. That will then be your major contribution in rebuilding our civilisation.

---

[14] https://www.mannwest.com/wp-content/uploads/2023/04/Hoover-Statecraft-and-Classical-Liberal-Reforms_220202.pptx

PART 4

AUSTRALIA AT THE CROSSROADS 2024

So, with our eyes firmly focused on Australia, which 'Road Ahead' should we choose?

Our goal should be to maximize our success in creating a peaceful and productive nation, worthy of universal respect.

In 2023, following an excruciating campaign, 60% of Australian voters decided against changes to our Constitution.

The expensive Constitutional campaign was designed to divide our nation along racial lines, bringing to an end Australia's great example of many nations and many languages uniting as Australia.

However, every step of this dismemberment has been carefully achieved by our Prime Minister Albanese and his assembled team.

Never under-estimate a Trotskyite from his earlier Sydney University days. Someone who has studied Marxist – Gramscian – Alinsky strategies.

He was strategically one step ahead all the way.

His clear understanding of the importance of dividing the nation, the business community and even the families, to the point where we no longer have any cohesive belief system.

Into that vacuum it is so easy to insert Marxist Socialism and recruit more battalions of individuals who become reliant on endless government hand-outs.

To ensure success of such a plan, it is vital to recruit thousands of 'useful idiots' (a Leninist – Marxist term – later used by Stalin).

All those signatories from big business, big education, big entertainment, who usually describe themselves as 'elites' are beholden to big government, as recipients of subsidies, grants, and favours of some kind.

Fortunately, the 'non-elites' or in Aussie terms 'the average punters' can recognize corruption when they see it.

It was no co-incidence that the P.M. posed with the Qantas CEO and the freshly painted 'Yes!' on the Qantas plane, on the very same day that this government knocked back Qatar's application to compete by flying an additional 21 regular flights into Australia, every week. (Currently 28 flights per week).

How do the shareholders of Australia's big banks, the big companies and big charitable foundations feel about their companies (yes, the shareholders do own the companies) donating countless millions of dollars to woke causes they disagree with?

Will we see some class actions taken, to declare that these directors, in a swift return to Good Corporate Governance, could now be forced to personally repay the funds that they have frivolously squandered?

Perhaps the average Aussie Punter holds our Constitution in higher regard than we hold our politicians. The Constitution is really there to protect us from our politicians, and we should think carefully before we tamper with it.

Meanwhile, instead of this ostentatious display currently on view of what 'bad losers' look like, this is surely the time to focus on ensuring that the existing torrent of welfare dollars gets through to those genuinely in need, instead of 'getting lost' in the giant sponge of the Welfare Industry.

How to create a Socialist State
By Saul Alinsky

There are eight levels of control that must be obtained before you are able to create a socialist state. The first is the most important.

1) Healthcare–Control healthcare and you control the people

2) Poverty–Increase the Poverty level as high as possible, poor people are easier to control and will not fight back if you are providing everything for them to live.
3) Debt--Increase the debt to an unsustainable level. That way you are able to increase taxes, and this will produce more poverty.
4) Gun Control--Remove people's ability to defend themselves from the Government. That way you are able to create a police state.
5) Welfare–Take control of every aspect of their lives (Food, Housing, and Income)
6) Education–Take control of what people read and listen to - take control of what children learn in school. Think: "Common Core"
7) Religion--Remove the belief in God from the Government and schools.
8) Class Warfare--Divide the people into the wealthy and the poor. This will cause more discontent and it will be easier to take (Tax) the wealthy with the support of the poor.

These are certainly interesting times, and I am more convinced, than ever, that government, whilst masquerading as your friend, is anything but.

Despite imposing so many self-made crises upon us, I am convinced there is no crisis at all other than a leadership crisis (both in business and politics).

All these fabricated crises are reasons to institute programs. As you know, it is only in a crisis, that change can be imposed upon us and, when that crisis occurs the actions that are taken depends upon the ideas that are lying around at that time.

That is why Mannkal's role in generating ideas that can be picked up and used is more important than ever.

It would take a full book to list the current crises presented in the daily media, ranging from climate to housing affordability, to energy and phasing out reliable sources of energy and replacing them with intermittent energy. So, the list goes on.

Governments cannot solve these problems as their approach is inevitably to try and make this problem permanent – it gives them safety and security for their own future.

For the government, when they see people falling off the cliff (so to speak), their solution is to provide ambulances at the bottom of the cliff. The solution that people, such as yourselves, would see instead is to 'fence off the cliff top'.

Defending the free market in terms of economics is easy.

That is what the Mannkal Foundation was originally set up to do. Socialism sounded good in theory, but in practice it did not work, and under-privileged people received the worst deal of all!

This was proven decisively in 1990 when the Soviet Union imploded (I know, I was there). Then from the ruins, the intellectuals of the Socialist-Fabians gathered together and meticulously redesigned a system to get themselves out of this embarrassing situation.

Their new system involved dropping the name 'Communism' and adopting the new name of 'Social Democrats'.

Let me tell you about another time where I just happened to be on the spot when these changes were being finalised. If you were present at the Socialist International Conference in Sydney, Australia, in March 1991, you would have seen me there in the back row fitted up like all the other delegates with the mobile earpiece translating device.

I had difficulty getting in without documentation, but when interrogated by the gaunt-faced registration attendant I admitted to being a 'poet of the revolution'.

She still wanted to see my identification documents but accepted my reply that 'poets of the revolution don't carry identification'.

My interest in attending was simply to see what they had planned for us.

You would have seen the President of Socialist International, Willy Brandt the former Chancellor of West Germany, along with Gough Whitlam, Bob Hawke, Gareth Evans and other prominent members of the Australian Labor Party and you would have followed the general discussion that as Communism was generally seen to be losing credibility around the world and their switch to the word Socialism was also losing credibility. They had now redefined their plan under the general terms of 'social democracy' and all the various Communist Parties in the countries, represented at that conference now called themselves 'Social Democrats'.

In fact, in some of those East European countries the word Communism was in such low esteem that the Communist Party by that name had been outlawed – but of course the communist bureaucracy lived on and was keen to expand membership – so they devised a new recruiting scheme. Members who recruited one new member were excused from membership fees for a year. Members who recruited two new members no longer needed to remain members themselves. Those who recruited three new members were presented with an engraved silver plaque which stated that they were never members in the first place.

They may have changed their name, but they had not changed their philosophy, and it is the consistency of their philosophy that has enabled them to do so much damage.

Australia's Gough Whitlam was a raging success when measured by their standards. He transformed Australia in the vision of H.C. Coombs and the other back-room socialists so that over the three years of Whitlam rule although productivity rose only 1%, wages rose 70%, the size of the public service rose 12.6%, parliamentary salaries increased by 36%, Federal spending by 80% and inflation to 20%.

He had bought the minds and souls of the public sector and their hangers-on who by 1991 represented one in three of those termed employed as defined by our official statistics.

Ever since that time, March 1991, the Communists/Socialists, have been too smart to fight us on economic terms (that is the battle they lost).

They have been fighting us on cultural/philosophical terms designed to destroy traditional Western Culture, even to the point of destroying our language so that now, what was regressive, is now called progressive. Their use of the word 'progressive', is exactly the opposite to progress, as we know it.

No wonder they have won the culture wars with ESG (Environmental, Social and Governance) and DEI (Diversity, Equity and Inclusion) and their Woke agenda. We were still fighting the economic wars.

By decimating our culture, they have weakened us to the point that our standards, in just about everything, have slipped against international standards, when measured against non-tainted countries.

Through the adoption of these programs, our so-called leaders chased most industries out of Australia, including the car industry.

Good luck with manufacturing nuclear submarines! But let us not get side-tracked. My point is that Mannkal's focus, once one hundred percent directed toward economics has now a deeply embedded mix of culture, ethics, and economics, in our modest attempt to undo the damage of the past 30 years.

That is the healthy mix that you will see if you track the career paths of the many Mannkal scholars as they step forward to play a part in Australia's future.

So many people who I speak with are aware of the need for Australia to lift its game, and they ask me, "what can we do?" Let me lead up to making some suggestions on how we can become effective 'activists for good', by first stating the obvious.

For us to 'do nothing' will lead us simply to more of the same life-threatening inertia.

If we decide to be part of the solution instead of being part of the problem, there are choices ahead of us on 'which road to take'.

Fresh thinking, to approach these various problems, from a different angle creates our best chance for change, equally applicable whether we are talking change for a country, a company, or an individual.

Let me give you an example of 'fresh thinking' as being part of your 'road ahead'.

For seven years of my life I was 'on hold' during a dispute with the Australian Taxation Office (ATO), employing the best lawyers and getting nowhere.

An American lawyer (who I 'bumped into' by accident) had a quick look at my situation and said, "Ron, you will never get anywhere using the law, as your Tax Act is written in an ambiguous fashion. You must elevate your case to a Constitutional matter where they will understand that in the case of any law being ambiguous, because it was not written in an ambiguous fashion by the citizens, must be interpreted on the side of the citizen."

Upon his advice we proceeded and solved the problem in one day! Yes, seven years wasted, and a solution discovered in one day.

Similar fresh thinking is now required to get Australia back to working effectively and we can start with some flexible employment laws that could once again bring industry back to Australia and reverse the current trend of 'offshoring' our employment opportunities.

I can think of no more noble cause to which we could apply our intellect.

BE AN ACTIVIST!
Much more fun than being a spectator!

Having decided to become an activist, you could select which of the 'four roads ahead' fit your talents and passions.

Each 'road' can be effective but there will be one that takes you forward in perfectly pitched harmony. Just as in music, you will know when you have made the right choice. Instead of the correct selection of notes, you will have the right mix, and no-one else can guide you with this selection.

I see the four roads as follows:-

• **Education** (as being a precondition for any meaningful increase in freedom).

• **Economic self-protection and self-preservation**.
How individuals can protect themselves against inflation and other government policies. Always remember that if you get 'wiped out' you are of little use to anyone.

• **Non-violence, peaceful forms of civil disobedience** (against governments and bureaucrats when they go beyond their legitimate functions). I always remember the wise words of Ayn Rand, "They can only do to you what you permit them to do."

- **Political action and its use to roll back the power of the State and restore the rights of individuals.**

May I expand on these 'four roads ahead?'

- **Education** has been my own choice, following a short but energetic sojourn into politics… but more on that later.

Education is important in developing the partnership of freedom and self-responsibility. These are interchangeable terms as self-responsibility is impossible unless one be free, and one cannot be free if not self-responsible.

As mentioned in an earlier chapter my first mentor, Leonard E. Read, suggested that education is a civilized alternative to ramming ideas down the throats of others. Instead, if we have a good idea, just work on it. If it is any good, others will then borrow it from us.

This is the 'road ahead', for our Mannkal Foundation. The philosopher Eric Hoffer once wrote, "The central task of education is to implant a will and facility for learning; it should produce not learned but learning people."

- **Economic self-protection and self-preservation**.

It sounds simple and logical that we will always make decisions that will protect ourselves from inflation and other government policies.

But, this is not the case as many of these damaging policies are 'sold to us' by politicians, as being to our benefit.

A short course in the vital branch of economics called 'Public Choice Theory' will alert you to how legislation is drafted in favour of those few who receive the concentrated benefits (they have much to gain so will work the hardest to lobby for this legislation).

The high costs of such legislation are always designed to be spread over a large number of people. These large number of people will carry that burden as it is not 'life threatening'.

What is 'life threatening' is the multitude of such burdens. Financial illiteracy will guarantee that your later years will not be your best years.

If you are successful with your economic self-protection and self-preservation 'journey' you will always have sufficient funds to defend yourself and to contribute in support of your allies on the educational and political 'roads ahead'.

• The third 'road ahead' is that of **non-violent, peaceful forms of civil disobedience** (against government and bureaucrats when they go beyond their legitimate functions).

This is the 'road' requiring that delicate balance between courage and wisdom.

• Courage is less about what you're not afraid of and more about what you are afraid of but are willing to face.

- Wisdom is less about what you know and more about what you know you don't know.

This particular 'road' is by far the most interesting and deserves a more detailed treatment than this brief exploratory trip. It is one that may lead you to study the several excellent country comparisons.

- The Fraser Institute's 'Economic Freedom of the World' – *www.freetheworld.com*
- The Heritage Foundation's 'Index of Economic Freedom' – *https://www.heritage.org/index/*

It may lead you to obtaining E-Residency for Estonia and other countries with far more welcoming business environments than Australia.

It may lead you to reading the inspirational works of Henry David Thoreau who inspired other protestors, such as Gandhi, Mandela, and Martin Luther King.

It may lead you to read the incredible literature of peaceful revolt.

I will mention only two such books, from our library:- *The Rebel* by Albert Camus (winner of the Noble Prize for Literature, 1957). This is a classic essay on revolution. For Camus, the urge to revolt is one of the 'essential dimensions' of human nature. As old regimes, throughout the world collapse, is it inevitable that revolution leads to tyranny?

The other book by Albert O. Hirschmann *Exit, Voice, and Loyalty* is a collection of responses to the decline in firms, organizations, and states.

If we are loyal, how much should we speak up before we exit?

Anyone who is disgusted at political or corporate antics will bond with Hirschmann, who in his introduction says, "Each society learns to live with a certain amount of such dysfunctional or mis-behaviour; but lest the misbehaviour feed on itself and lead to general decay, society must be able to marshal from within itself forces which will make as many of the faltering actors as possible revert to the behaviour required for its proper functioning."

This 'road' should be navigated with great care as those less brave will envy your courage and spirit of adventure.

Always remember that the occasional revolt is a very good thing, as Thomas Jefferson said, "When the government fears the people, there is liberty; when the people fear the government, there is tyranny."

- And the fourth 'road' **political action and its use to roll back the power of the 'state' and restore the rights of individuals.**

My own brief sojourn into politics was with nine other Australians in 1974, we formed the Workers Party / Progress Party and that interesting experiment was covered in a chapter, 'Our Very Own Political Party'... see Heroic Misadventures link to free eBook –

https://www.mannwest.com/books/heroic-misadventures/

This political 'road' starts with a careful study of 'just what is the legitimate role of government?'

It is not easy to answer this question, and that degree of difficulty is deliberate! For us to say that 'we are not interested in government or politics' would only be a good answer if government or politics would leave us alone, so there is every reason to step inside this murky mess (or as Donald Trump calls it 'the swamp').

Way back, in 1977, when I was still drawn to the political path, I 'booked' what was then called a 'long distance trunk line telephone call' to Antony Fisher (see earlier chapter). Fisher, in the United Kingdom, had founded the Institute of Economic Affairs and his political influence fascinated me, hence my telephone call to enthusiastically encourage Fisher to visit Australia.

Although he did say that he intended to visit, I don't think he ever managed a visit as my various personal meetings with him were always elsewhere.

Our telephone call was long (in those days interrupted every three minutes with 'warning beeps') and as I had several questions for him, with his permission, I recorded his responses. I then transcribed his comments about 'bringing economic principles to politics'.

His method consisted of completing thoroughly researched studies and making the resultant information freely available to politicians; intellectuals, the media and other avenues through which the public are normally 'educated'.

He explained the need for these studies as follows:- "One self-imposed trouble of politicians is that they are very busy and have little, if any, time for research. MPs have an impossible job when government becomes involved in every detail of our lives. Laws reach the statute book without proper discussion. This result is inevitable so long as parliament is trying to do work which no parliament can ever do.

The average politician does little or no research, and without a sound understanding of principles he is unlikely to be constructive. It is easy to be negative and easiest of all for a politician in opposition to be critical when the ruling party has been in government long enough to have proved itself no better than the last. This is why politicians spend much time attacking each other and the public get bored with the process."

"Research publications issued by a political parties are bound to be biased, and therefore attract little attention for the press and the intellectual world. The many political compromises in producing a 'package deal' will probably mean that the parties cannot resist increasing taxation and government action, thereby helping to build up the syndrome which is so harmful. Because government decision-making is not based on principles, an inevitable result is that countless 'deals' are made to meet the demands of pressure groups. As each group seeks to achieve privileges at the expense of others, and as all the others are doing exactly the same, the ultimate result must be a highly uneconomic system based on restraint and compulsion. Lacking fundamental principles as guides, the politician and his party organisation are like amateur explorers marching in step to an unknown destination without a map, navigational equipment of any real knowledge of the stars."

"The politician is apt to be an avid reader of the press. He wishes to gauge 'public opinion' as a way of winning or holding on to power, prestige and votes. Yet so long as he hopes to become a leader by being a follower, he must eventually fail. To be a leader requires an understanding of fundamental ideas and how to put them into practice."

"The success of new ideas depends on at least one person not only understanding the case, but also writing it down for others to study. If the report is convincing and preferably has a good summary, and perhaps even a summary of a summary, it will be read, reviewed, and increasingly taught to others. In due time, it will begin to produce consequences."

"As politicians become less sure of themselves, and less able to offer any alternative policy which has not already been discredited, many would wrongly welcome a coalition. The fashionable fear of not wishing to 'abdicate responsibilities to the free market' will obstruct a move in the right direction."

Now, you will understand why I have always regarded Antony Fisher as the 'most successful politician, never to have entered parliament'.

No discussion of politics would be complete without reference to our Constitution.

I often regret that so few Australians have had sufficient exposure to our Constitution and the opportunity to compare ours with other constitutions. Let me encourage you to join the Samuel Griffith Society –
https://www.samuelgriffith.org/

Constitutions can be judged by whether they promote liberty or violate it. My friend Sheldon Richman puts it well, in his book *America's Counter-Revolution* – "What is a constitution typically thought to be? Aside from a blueprint of the government, it is thought to be a set of restraints on the conduct of government officials. Remember, Alexander Hamilton and other Federalists said the proposed Constitution was by *nature* a bill of rights, or a set of restraints on the government. Officials, they argued, may not do what they were not authorized to do by the constitution."

CONCLUSION

Thank you for your patience in coming all this way with me, on this journey, leading to the four forks in the road, and pausing briefly until the most appropriate selection has been made by you.

AFTERWORD

When I finished the above chapter at 3.00 a.m. on April 14, 2024 I had an immediate and impromptu flash-back to an earlier experience.

After working a similar 'late shift' on a long piece, covering our mining industry, I sat back and for no particular reason asked myself, "What would Shakespeare think of our mining industry?" and produced this following piece:– *https://www.mannwest.com/what-would-shakespeare-think-of-our-mining-industry/*

My mind was similarly scrambled last night when I asked myself, "What would Robert Frost think of these four road alternatives, compared with his simpler choice of two roads?"

Frost would probably have said to me, "Now listen here Ron; I hope your readers don't misunderstand your four road concept as much as my readers have with my much simpler choice.

My readers are even confused by the name of my poem, which is 'The Road Not Taken', even though most of them refer to the poem as 'The Road Less Travelled."

But, more importantly, I hope your readers realize how fortunate they are to have a choice between four such roads?

There are not many countries in this world where these choices and opportunities are as 'open' as in Australia.

Each of those four choices also has the potential to take you on to success.

So, hasten toward your objective of maximizing your freedoms, before it is too late!"

ACKNOWLEDGEMENTS

I cannot claim one hundred percent credit for bringing this book to conclusion so, would like to thank, among many, the following four:

- Nicola Wright, Mannkal's CEO, who suggested the structure and got us rolling.
- Judy Carroll, my Executive Assistant for the mammoth task of bringing all these scattered thoughts together.
- John Ogilvie for the front and rear cover design.
- Jenny, my understanding wife, for keeping up the constant flow of cheese, crackers, and coffee to keep me awake during the final late night edit sessions.

Machiavelli and the Globalists: *https://brownstone.org/articles/machiavelli-globalists-why-elites-despise-independent-thought/?utm_medium=onesignal&utm_source=push*

The Prince – Niccolo Machiavelli, *https://www.amazon.com.au/gp/product/0141442255/ref=dbs_a_def_rwt_hsch_vapi_tu00_p1_i1*

Management and Machiavelli – Antony Jay: *https://www.amazon.com.au/Management-Machiavelli-Jay/dp/0893842605/ref=sr_1_4?crid=1S8O0EO485TGI&keywords=Management+and+Machiavelli&qid=1680763833&s=books&sprefix=management+and+machiavelli%2Cstripbooks%2C327&sr=1-4*

New Machiavelli – Alistair McAlpine: *https://www.amazon.com.au/New-Macchiavelli-Hb-Alistair-McAlpine/dp/1854104713/ref=sr_1_3?crid=282WWIH805MBT&keywords=The+New+Machiavelli+Renaissance+-Realpolitik+for+modern+managers&qid=1680763966&s=books&sprefix=the+new+machiavelli+renaissance+realpolitik+for+modern+manage%2Cstripbooks%2C269&sr=1-3*

The Seven Books on the Art of War – Niccolo Machiavelli: *https://www.amazon.com/Seven-Books-Art-War/dp/1545129096*

Also from Ron Manners:-

- *So I Headed West* – *W.G. Manners*. Ballarat to Broken Hill, to Kanowna, to Kalgoorlie. "When miners were heroes" 1863-1924.
- *Kanowna's Barrowman* – *James Balzano*. The early history of Kalgoorlie Goldrushes – (with George Compton).
- *Never A Dull Moment*. Kalgoorlie's golden years through to the seventies, including life in the World War I trenches – (with Charles & Nancy Manners).
- *Heroic Misadventures (Australia: Four Decades – Full Circle)*; 1970-2009.
- *The Lonely Libertarian (Turning Ideas into Gold – Then Gold into Ideas)*.
- *Poems of Passion (A prospector's poetic soul)*.
- *Mannerisms* (1985-2020).

All available for purchase or as free e-books @

https://www.mannwest.com/books/

INDEX

Acker Bilk, 59, 60
Adam Smith, 113
Al Gore, 105
Albert Camus, 132
Albert O Hirschmann, 132
Antonio Gramsci, 101, 109
Antony Fisher, x, 2, 41-44, 50, 51, 63, 134, 137
Aristotle, 9, 23
Atlas Network, 2, 44, 63, 66, 76, 112
Australian Labor Party, 105, 124
Austrian Economics Center, 87
Ayn Rand, 17, 129

Bali, 21
Benny Goodman, 60
Berlin Wall, 14
Bert Kelly, 110
Bob Anderson, 58
Bob Hawke, 110, 111, 124
Bratislava, 89, 99
Buckingham Palace, 24

Canberra, 3, 4, 31, 81
Centre for Independent Studies, 34
Checkan, 38
China, 100, 109
Clarinet, 53, 55-60
Climate Collapse, 105
Coal, 100, 101, 104
Commonwealth Study Conference, 2, 25, 26, 29, 30

Communism, x, 19, 123, 124
Conservationists, 106
D.E.I., 98, 99
Dave Shore, 58
Dr Johnson, viii

E.S.G., 97-99
Ed Crane, 39
Egg Marketing Board, 44
Electric Vehicles, 106
Energy Security, 106
Energy Transition, 107
Entrepreneurs, 35, 89, 90, 95, 97, 98
Eric Hoffer, 130
Esperance, 26, 35, 52, 55, 56
Estonia, 78, 89, 99, 132
Exchange Hotel, 58-60

F.A. Hayek, vi, ix, x, 1, 2, 32-40, 43, 45, 50
Freeman Magazine, 7, 11, 49
Free-Market Road Show, 73

Gandhi, 132
Gareth Evans, 124
Gas, 101, 105, 107, 108
George Koether, 39
George Orwell, 19
Gough Whitlam, 124, 125
Green Party, 105
Greg Dawson, 58
Guatemala, 1, 83

H.C. Coombs, 125
Hans F. Sennholz, 113
Henry David Thoreau, 132
Heroic Humility, 45
Heroic Misadventures, 51, 96, 133, 134
Hong Kong, 34, 109
Hugh Hefner, 16
Humility, x, 9

Inflation, 32, 125, 129, 130
Institute of Economic Affairs, 2, 29, 44, 134
Institute of Public Affairs, 73
Isaac Newton, 80
Istanbul, 64, 65

James Buchanan, 77
James Walker, 84
Jaycees (Junior Chamber), 50
Jenny Manners, 14, 38
John Hospers, x, 2, 14, 15, 20-23, 25, 29, 49
John Hyde, 110-112
John Maynard Keynes, 37

Kalgoorlie, 7, 8, 52, 53, 56, 58, 59, 75, 76
Kalgoorlie School of Mines, 8
Kalgoorlie Town Hall, 59
Keele University, 28
Kiruna, 94
Kyiv, 66, 89, 109

Laurie Morrow, vii
Laverton, 53, 54, 60
Leonard Read, viii, ix, 2, 10, 12, 30
Libertarian International, 19
Libertarian Party, 15, 17
Lord Acton, vii
Ludwig von Mises, 35, 113

Maidan Youth Revolution, 66
Mandela, 132
Manhattan Institute, 44, 105
Mannkal Economic Education Foundation, v, ix, 10, 29
Mannkal Scholars, 2-5, 126
Margaret Thatcher, 64, 65, 68
Mark P. Mills, 105
Martin Luther King, 132
Maryan Zablotskyy, 112
Monday Conference, 33, 34
Mont Pelerin Society, 1-4, 12, 32, 64, 83, 84, 114

National Electricity Market, 102
New Hebrides, 19

Paradise Lost, viii
Peter Iancov, 106
Phillip Lynch, 50
Playboy, 16, 49
Poems of Passion, 68, 70-72, 80
Poet of the revolution, 123

Poland, 100, 109
"Pom Pom" Stevens, 52, 53, 79
President Yanukovych, 64
President Zelenskyy, 63, 79
Prince Philip Duke of Edinburgh, 25-31, 50
Prof. Nils Karlson, 114
Progressive, 125
Project Western Australia, 76, 112
Public Choice Theory, vii, 77, 98, 105, 131
Pucinellia, 27

Rafe Champion, 33
Ratio Institute of Sweden, 114
Reece Withers, 104
Regressive, 125
Robert Frost, 139
Robert Stevens, 79
Roger Douglas, 110
Roger Kerr, 109
Ron Kitching, 32, 33
Ronald Reagan Presidential Library, 20
Russia, 39, 60, 67, 73, 74, 77, 78, 100, 107, 112
Ruth Richardson, 110

Samuel Griffith Society, 137
Sarah Basden, 24
Saul Alinsky, 119
Seatside Companion, 91, 92
Senator Dorothy Tangney, 26
Shakespeare, 139
Sheldon Richman, 137

Sir John Cowperthwaite, 109
Social Democrats, 123, 124
Socialist International, 123, 124
Socialist-Fabians, 123
Sophiyka, 69, 70
Soviet Union, 78, 113, 123
Sweden, 94

The Fraser Institute, 132
The Heritage Foundation, 132
The Road to Serfdom, 36, 37, 43
Thomas Sowell, 61
Timken, 7, 10
Tom Palmer, 112
Tom Peters, 1
Turkey, 27, 65, 93

Ukraine, 63, 64, 67-69, 73, 74, 76, 78, 79, 109, 112
University Francisco Marroquin (UFM), 1
University of Western Australia, 15, 49

Vanuatu, 20
Vasyl Myroshnychenko, 79
Volvo, 94

Warsaw, 89, 109
Western Civilisation, 80
Willy Brandt, 124
Woke, 120, 125
Woodside, 103, 104

Yuliya, 64-69, 74, 82, 84